CLEOPATRA'S NOSE

CLEOPATRA'S NOSE

Essays on the Unexpected

DANIEL J. BOORSTIN

Edited by RUTH F. BOORSTIN

*The best qualification of a prophet
is to have a good memory.*
— MARQUESS OF HALIFAX

VINTAGE BOOKS

A Division of Random House, Inc.   New York

FIRST VINTAGE BOOKS EDITION, NOVEMBER 1995

Grateful acknowledgment is made to the Edna St. Vincent Millay
Society and Elizabeth Barnett, literary executor, for permission
to reprint six lines from " Upon this age, that never speaks its mind,"
by Edna St. Vincent Millay. From Collected Poems, HarperCollins.
Copyright © 1939, 1969 by Edna St. Vincent Millay
and Norma Millay Ellis. Reprinted by permission
of Elizabeth Barnett, literary executor.

The Library of Congress has cataloged the Random House
edition as follows: Boorstin, Daniel J. (Daniel Joseph).
Cleopatra's Nose / by Daniel J. Boorstin :
edited by Ruth F. Boorstin. — 1st ed.
p. cm.
Includes bibliographical references and index.
ISBN 0-679-43505-0
1. Civilization, Modern—History.
2. Science—History. 3. Science and civilization.
I. Boorstin, Ruth Frankel.
II. Title.
CB358.B63 1994
909—dc20   94-1079
Vintage ISBN: 978-0-679-75518-0

To our grandchildren,
Couriers of the Unexpected

Foreword

"Cleopatra's nose, had it been shorter," Pascal speculated, "the whole face of the world would have been changed." When we focus on turning points in history we recognize the crucial role of the accidental and the trivial. We have no doubt that the personal charms and vices of Caesar, Queen Elizabeth, Napoleon, Disraeli, Hitler, Stalin, FDR, and JFK have shaped events. But we are reluctant to believe that the future will be as full of surprises as the past. Even the unpredicted sudden collapse of the Soviet empire has not chastened us, and we go on confidently predicting the course of democracy and the world.

These essays of the last few years explore some of the surprising novelties and unexpected continuities in our recent past. How has technology opened new realms of ignorance and given our times a claim to be the age of negative discovery? How has our nation, celebrated for material successes, come to be troubled by a new obsession with the inner world of conscience? How did the printing press make our Constitution possible? And how did New World technology provide us with a capitol of classical design with a cast-iron dome? The piquant contrast between Tocqueville's America and Custine's Russia gives us some clues to history's claim to be the cautionary science.

The fourth kingdom, the machine kingdom where we live, reveals how popular expectations inherited from the sciences have been frustrated. How can we come to terms with the need for the unnecessary and the deepening paradoxes of science in a time of the increasing political power of common sense? All of which adds up, from diverse times and places, and especially from the American experience, to the perils of prophecy—which our American optimism might prefer to call the delights of the unexpected.

Contents

REALMS OF DISCOVERY

Upon this gifted age, in its dark hour,
Falls from the sky a meteoric shower
Of facts. . . . they lie unquestioned, uncombined.
Wisdom enough to leech us of our ill
Is daily spun; but there exists no loom
To weave it into fabric. . . .

—Edna St. Vincent Millay, *Huntsman, What Quarry*

1

The Age of Negative Discovery

When Albert Einstein was asked about forty years ago how the West had come to the idea of scientific discovery, he gave a simple answer. "Development of Western Science," he explained, "is based on two great achievements, the invention of the formal logical system (in Euclidean geometry) by the Greek philosophers, and the discovery of the possibility to find out causal relationship by systematic experiment (Renaissance). In my opinion one has not to be astonished that the Chinese sages have not made these steps. The astonishing thing is that these discoveries were made at all." Einstein was surely correct in seeing scientific discovery as an institution of Western culture. His characteristically simple explanation, however, does not take account of the remarkable transformations of the venture of discovery in this century.

The works of discovery in every age shape—and shake up—the thinking of the whole literate community. And this effect has multiplied with the rise of democracy and of literacy. The familiar example, of course, is how the works of Copernicus (1473–1543) and his followers disturbed Western culture with the realization that the earth was no longer the center. More recent examples are the impact of Darwinian biology and Freudian psychology. Nowadays, the space sciences, arcane and specialized though they have become, continue to have a profound and wide influence on the whole community's thinking.

We in the lay community continue to reach for the meanings of scientific discoveries that are beyond our layman's understanding. We enjoy having our imagination titillated. How otherwise can we account for one of the most remarkable publishing phenomena of recent times? Stephen Hawking's short but difficult *Brief History of Time: From the Big Bang to Black Holes* (1988) has entered the *Guinness Book of World Records* for the longest period (four years) of any book on the British best-seller list, and with a sale of some five million copies. We have seen the wide and enduring popular interest in the readable tales of Jules Verne and H. G. Wells, in the charming personality of ET and his tribe, in the science fiction of Isaac Asimov and Arthur Clarke, and even in older serious works like those of James Jeans and Arthur Eddington, and in the current writings of Herbert Friedman.

Nowadays public interest in discovery is greater than ever. But the role of the discoverer in the space sciences has been transformed, with novel consequences for the thinking of laymen like me.

For the modern realm of discovery in the space sciences our prototypes should not be the familiar heroes of the so-called Great Age of Discovery—Leif Eriksson, Columbus, Cortés, Magellan, Drake. Our proper prototype, instead, is the prosaic, less romanticized Captain James Cook (1728–1779). He has not had his due in the annals of discovery. This may be a common fate of negative discoverers. Of them, Captain Cook was perhaps the greatest. You will recall that he earned his place in the chronicles of seafaring by proving that the fabled Great Southern Continent did not exist. That fabled land was supposed to reach up from the Antarctic toward Southeast Asia, making the Indian Ocean a lake. We are inclined to forget or underestimate the difficulty of negative discovery. For it is far easier to encounter some new island or even an unexpected new continent than to prove that some long-admired fixture of the imagination does not exist. To put a new land, a new passageway on the map one needed only to go there, and happily surprise the world with a new presence.

But to prove a negative, even if the logicians had not insisted that it was theoretically impossible, is an exhausting enterprise. It demands the exploring and discarding of all imaginable possibilities. Negative discovery is also much less welcome than an act of simple affirmative discovery. People don't like to have their imaginations unfurnished. The legendary Great South Land, which Cook erased from the map, had been a promising field of empire, with natural wealth of incalculable value. It remained so, as long as it was never found.

To prove that the Great South Land did *not* exist was not only an unwelcome disillusion, it required one of the most terrifying sea voyages in history. Leaving England in July 1772, Captain Cook did not return till July 1775. With two newly built Whitby colliers, the *Resolution* (462 tons) and the *Adventure* (340 tons), he came down around the Cape of Good Hope, reached 71°10′ South, traversed the whole southernmost rim of the Pacific in the Antarctic regions, then into the Atlantic toward the Cape of Good Hope and back up to England. This was no voyage through any becalmed Sargasso Sea, but one teetering on the edge of Antarctic ice, overshadowed and threatened by crackling and crumbling iceberg-alps.

Captain Cook's instructions took account of both possibilities—that the continent did or did not exist. If he found any part of it he had orders from the Admiralty to survey it, claim it for Britain, and distribute medals to the natives. Officers and crew were to observe strict secrecy about the voyage, and all logs and journals were to be confiscated after the ship's return. In this, one of the greatest, and surely one of the longest, discovery voyages in history, Cook sailed more than seventy thousand miles. Never before had there been so long a voyage with one focused inquiring purpose. Not to plant a new colony, not to seek an Eldorado, nor find gold or silver or precious gems, nor capture slaves. Cook had made his earlier voyage to Tahiti—also a brilliant feat of navigation—for astronomical observations of the transit of Venus, on June 3, 1769. Now his grand success with the *Resolution* and the *Adventure* was resounding testimony to the courage of the modern skeptical spirit. The Antarctic was dangerously different from the Arctic, of which Europeans had had some glimpses. The uncharted Antarctic, scenes of perpetual mountainous ice beyond the belief of temperate Europe, was a happy hunting ground for extravagant *a priori* speculation. And Cook's voyage itself would spark the ominous allegory of Coleridge's "Rime of the Ancient Mariner."

To scotch those ancient legends and speculations required a kind of discovering courage and passion that would characterize our modern age of negative discovery. This passion and courage and the sophisticated purpose of Cook, his crew, his expert naturalists and skilled astronomers were brilliantly summarized in the homely wisdom of Josh Billings (1818–1885): "It ain't what a man don't know as makes him a fool, but what he does know as ain't so."

There was a shining symbolism in Cook's whole career. Self-educated, as a young man he turned down an opportunity to command a ship, and chose instead to widen his knowledge of the sea as a volunteer able seaman in the British navy. Rapidly promoted, he became a master, and surveyed the St. Lawrence River before the fall of Quebec. He showed a practical man's experimental spirit in his sympathy for the newly improved Harrison and Kendall chronometers and was one of the first to prove the chronometer's utility as a navigational instrument. Incidentally he was ready to learn new ways of dealing with the scurvy, the curse of long voyages in his time, and astonished contemporaries by bringing back his *Resolution,* after his three-year voyage, without losing a single man to the disease. He fought the scurvy by enforcing cleanliness on board and trying new diets of orange, lemon, and their juices along with sauerkraut, onions, and grasses encountered en route. It was precisely this practical sense, this imaginative openness to new techniques, that would distinguish the great negative discoverers in the following centuries.

The history of Western science confirms the aphorism that the great menace to progress is not ignorance but the illusion of knowledge. I will now suggest why I see Captain Cook as the prototypical modern discovery hero. The negative discoverer is the historic dissolver of illusions. Perhaps we could call ours an age of negative discovery.

This feature of the realms of discovery in our age is conspicuous in the results of recent efforts to describe the universe. Marc Davis, Professor of Astronomy and Physics at the University of California, Berkeley, has provided us with a convenient summary. Here are the six main products of the progress of cosmology over the last four hundred years:

The Earth is *not* the center of the Universe.
The Sun is *not* the center of the Universe.
Our galaxy is *not* the center of the Universe.
Our type of matter is *not* the dominant constituent of the Universe (dark matter predominates instead).
Our Universe (seen and unseen) is *not* the only Universe.
Our physics is *not* the only physics. There might exist separate universes with completely different physics.

My poetic wife, Ruth, has eloquently suggested that this may make ours the Age of Gordian *Nots*.

In addition to these modern notions about space, there is also an equally modern view of time. On our distinctly modern menu of alternatives the experts offer us at least three different cosmological models:

Steady-state theory: The Universe is of infinite age; matter is continuously created at all times.

The Big Bang: The Universe is of finite age; matter and energy are conserved as the Universe expands.

Eternally inflating Big Bang: Our Universe has a finite age. The creation of all matter-energy in our Universe occurred at the end of the inflationary phase, when the incredible energy density of the false vacuum converted to ordinary matter and radiation.

All three possibilities are signposts to terra incognita. These propositions taken together provide what Professor Davis calls the Modern Creation Myth. This he deftly compresses into the notion that "the entire Universe we observe, and unimaginably far beyond, was created out of a single tiny vacuum fluctuation having zero energy content at an incredibly early time. . . . our entire Universe was quite literally created out of nothing." And Davis, in the modern spirit, instead of pursuing the heavy theological implications, concludes with Alan Guth's unforgettable suggestion that "the Universe is the ultimate free lunch."

How have we come to this vast and tantalizing expansion of terra incognita, to include the whole universe and our place in it? Professor Davis himself has succinctly described the triumphs of modern Western science as experiments in cosmology. These, I will suggest, are not simply the fruitful work of bold individual scientists. They are a by-product of large cultural and institutional changes of the last century, of processes that are accelerating and are likely to continue to accelerate. Put quite simply, they are a consequence of the application of developed technology to the processes of scientific discovery and the rise of the mechanized observer. The momentous consequence, which increases the scope and the realms of negative discovery, is a changed relation of data to meaning. Before the age of the mechanized observer, there was a tendency for meaning to outrun data. The modern tendency is quite the contrary, as we see data outrun meaning.

It is of course no accident that the heavens, where man had no direct personal experience, was the realm of the gods. Fertile in myth and legend, that unexplored realm was supposed to be rich in meaning for life on earth. Until the nineteenth century the data of space outside the earth were filtered through the interests and capacities of the human observer. The telescope and the microscope have, to be sure, extended, broadened, and deepened our human faculties of vision. But these are only tools, extensions of the human bodily senses. A machine is something else—a device that can be activated by forces outside the human body, bringing data not accessible to the unmechanized human body. The crucial new element is that the discoverer is no longer simply confronted by nature, by the data accessible to the person. Man creates machines, and the machines create data. Here are infinitely expanding new realms to be explored. Every new observing machine adds a new revelation of negative discovery, opening hitherto unrecognized areas of ignorance.

Some distinctive features of this modern realm of discovery were vividly revealed in the progress of *Voyager 2*, one of the most impressive and successful recent efforts to reach out beyond the solar system. The perceptive science reporter Stephen S. Hall has given us his eyewitness account of what happened at 9:00 P.M. on the evening of August 19, 1989, as the technology team, a dozen "postmodern helmsmen," gathered on the second floor of Building 264 of NASA's Jet Propulsion Laboratory in the San Gabriel foothills of Pasadena, California. *Voyager 2*, already twelve years into its journey, had so far accomplished its assignment perfectly in flying by Jupiter, Saturn, and Uranus. Within just five days it would, as Hall observed, "brush the treetops of Neptune and hurtle past Triton." The staff had met to agree on the radio adjustment of the rudder of the craft (2.7 billion miles away) to ensure its reaching the appointed target.

A map of the solar system on the wall showed where Neptune, traveling at 12,000 miles per hour around the sun, and *Voyager 2*, traveling at about 61,000 miles per hour, were to meet for the planned observation by the spacecraft. Beside it on the wall, a sign read, WE DO PRECISION GUESSWORK. While this familiar

chart of the solar system was visible, the navigational chart of
Voyager 2 remained out of sight inside the computers, continually revising as the voyage progressed. The JPL computers indicated that *Voyager* 2 would reach within one light-year of Sirius,
the Dog Star, in the year A.D. 359,000. Meanwhile, the achievements of *Voyager* 2 were sensational. On the morning of August
25, 1989, it provided images of Triton. *Voyager* 2 had traveled
some 4,429,508,700 miles during twelve years, and was now
being remotely guided to its intended target. It arrived five minutes ahead of the schedule that had been made years before, and
0.6 seconds later than its last advertised time. Its scientific product was some five trillion bits of data.

The road to this universe of the mechanized observer, of *Pioneers 10* and *11* and *Voyagers 1* and *2*, had been opened years
before by the application of photography to astronomy. The
mechanization of the telescope had made it possible to focus on
the desired object, and to enhance the human eye by exposing
photographic plates for hours building up images of faint objects and their spectra. By 1949 the Hale Telescope, the American astronomers' Big Eye, was being activated by a mere
one-twelfth-horsepower motor to follow the stars.

No longer was the patience and devotion of astronomers
tested by their willingness to keep their eyes glued to the telescope while they sat at high altitudes in the cold night after night
in electrically heated suits. Of course, that patience had paid off
in the works of intrepid astronomers like Milton Humason,
Edwin Hubble's collaborator, who spent some twenty-eight
years recording the spectral patterns of far-off galaxies to measure red shift. Gathering that data required that Humason first
find and fix on a faint nebulosity among the stars, then center
the image on the narrow slit of his spectrograph and hold it there
throughout the night. The plate would be kept from irrelevant
daylight and then the tedious observation would be repeated on
following nights. It was just such data for the momentous new

knowledge of red shift and of the nature and number of galaxies for Hubble's constant that exploded our view of the universe.

Only a century ago, in 1889, the precocious George Ellery Hale's new spectroheliograph opened the sun to new modes of exploration with new data, and with a technique applicable across the heavens. Improvements by Robert H. McMath revealed unexpected new realms of solar spicules. This was only one of a series of openings to new realms of our ignorance, which Herbert Friedman, a pioneer in rocket astronomy, properly labels the Invisible Universe. While the visible universe has limits, the Invisible Universe is, of course, limitless—and with it, too, countless new realms of negative discovery—ever outward to radio astronomy, the infrared, the ultraviolet, X-ray astronomy, to gamma rays, to the baffling neutrinos and endless new realms still unnamed.

In this age of negative discovery, of the mechanized observer, of machine-created data and ever newer kinds of data, we must note a new kind of momentum. Familiar enough is the momentum of knowledge, the ancient and perilous self-catalyzing quest for more knowledge, embodied in the parable of the apple and expulsion from the Garden of Eden. But the machine also has a momentum of its own.

The momentum of the technology of the mechanized observer is vividly illustrated in the Report of the National Research Council (from its Astronomy and Astrophysics Survey Committee in 1991) with a program and priorities for "The Decade of Discovery in the 1990's." The report calls for continued support for the great observatories and increased support for individual research grants. But the bulk of its recommendations, a prelude to its description of "Science Opportunities," gives priority to the "ground-based infrastructure" and calls for four "instrumental programs."

At the top of this list is the Space Infrared Telescope Facility (SIRTF), which would be "almost a thousand times more sensitive than earth-based telescopes operating in the infrared. Advanced arrays of infrared detectors would give SIRTF the ability to map complex areas and measure spectra a million times faster than any other space-borne infrared telescope." These would be based on the "technical heritage" of two successful Explorer missions. Closely following, to "draw on a decade of progress in the technology of building large mirrors," comes the proposal that "an infrared-optimized 8-m U.S. telescope operating on Mauna Kea, Hawaii, would provide a unique and powerful instrument for studying the origin, structure, and evolution of planets, stars, and galaxies." And then the "Millimeter Array (MMA) . . . of telescopes operating at millimeter wavelengths, would provide high-spatial and high-spatial-resolution images of star-forming regions and distant star-burst galaxies," which "would bring new classes of objects into clear view for the first time." But this is only the beginning of the list, followed by six "Moderate Programs," nine "Illustrative Small Programs," and nine space-based initiatives. All these come to an estimated cost for the decade of $3 billion 23 million.

The momentum of discovery-technology is further accelerated by two innovative techniques—adaptive optics and interferometry, "which promises spatial resolution better than a thousandth of an arc second by linking the outputs of widely separated telescopes." All this would be an extension to the spectacular Very Large Array, already in being. And there is the suggestion of improved instruments to detect neutrinos and "dark matter" (still so cryptic that it must be left in quotation marks). The momentum startles us with the final suggestion that "the chief advantage of the moon as a site for space astronomy is that it provides a large, solid foundation on which to build widely separated structures such as interferometers." Is this a promise to transform the whole solar system into an attractive novel base for interferometers focused on the universe?

For most of Western history interpretation has far outrun data. And there was an overwhelming and universal human temptation to ignore or discount data that menaced familiar and appealing interpretations. A well-known example is the reluctance of theologically oriented scientists in Galileo's day (1610) to accept the fact of sunspots, which his telescope had newly revealed. Some of the most respected men of learning refused to look through a device so diabolical that it purported to contradict Aristotle's appealing notion of the sun as the embodiment of unspotted fire, and even hint at imperfections in God's handiwork. The eminent Aristotelian scholar Cesare Cremonini said he would not waste his time looking through Galileo's contraption just to see what "no one but Galileo has seen . . . and besides, looking through those spectacles gives me a headache." Some even solaced themselves by saying that while Galileo's device might represent the facts here on earth, where it could be verified by experience, "in the sky it deceives us as some fixed stars are seen double." Father Clavius, professor of mathematics at the Collegio Romano, laughed at Galileo's four satellites of Jupiter, and said he could produce the same result if allowed a little time to build the images into some glasses. Galileo himself, wary of allowing novel facts to contradict familiar meanings, reported that after seeing an object magnified in his telescope he would again and again go up to the object to see that he had not been deceived.

So long as the aids to discovery were mere tools, extension of the bodily faculties, their products might be surprising or even shocking but were not unimaginable or unintelligible. The revisions of Ptolemaic into Copernican astronomy took centuries to secure acceptance, but the debate, even to the layman, was still intelligible. At worst the problems arose from what seemed the violations of common sense—such as the discovering that in fact heavy objects fell no more speedily than light objects, or the troubling suggestion that the solid, apparently static earth on which we stand is in fact in constant rotating motion. This became Galileo's own legendary dramatic affirmation of his discovery, when he reputedly stamped his foot, saying, "Anyway, it moves" *(Eppure, si muove!).*

But the development of the machinery of discovery of course allowed observations of which the unmechanized human body was incapable. The new data then extended and was limited only by the capacity of the machines—photography, spectrography, rocket astronomy, radio astronomy, and their successors. No longer bounded by the imagination of an observer fixing his telescope, the mechanized observer has been gathering whatever the proliferating machinery of discovery can report or record. A clue to the endless novelty of realms of discovery is the ever-enlarging vocabulary of discovery, with which even our best desk dictionaries can hardly keep pace. Every report of the progress of discovery must carry its own glossary of new terms and acronyms. Even the brief *Decade of Discovery* report of the National Research Council that I have mentioned carries a glossary of ten pages. Each new term is an omen of newly discovered areas of our ignorance. A familiar example is how Robert N. McMath's device for making time-lapse movies of the sun in hydrogen light gave us our first vision of spicules, with a new vision of the sun and hosts of new questions about the photosphere and chromosphere and the corona of the sun, all to be enriched and amplified in due course by the later data of X rays and the ultraviolet captured by rocket astronomy.

The momentum of invention and of proliferating technology accumulates data at a rate and in forms prescribed by the machines themselves. The ever-accelerating data provide hosts of answers to questions not yet asked. This challenges the discoverer with an ever-expanding task. No longer does he simply seek answers to conventional questions, nor demand that meager facts provide comforting cosmic meanings. Instead he tantalizes himself by making machines that pose new questions in uncharted oceans of expanding data. If a machine exists, or can be devised, it must be enlisted to produce data. We are not worried—perhaps not as much as we should be—that our twentieth-century Galileos are deceiving us by the data of machines. Instead we applaud all askers of unimagined questions, every reacher to negative discovery.

The mechanized observer would, of course, be vastly more productive of data than the human observer. Electronic imaging proved some two hundred times more sensitive than the photographic plates of the 1940s exposed to Hale's telescope. New uses of the silicon chip improved telescopes by a factor of 10 and silicon "pixels" yielded digitally readable data with a dynamic range of 1 million compared with a range of some 10 to 100 in a photographic emulsion. By 1978 the Charge Coupled Device (CCD) once again enormously multiplied the astronomer's research data. A single astronomical image made by a CCD required about 0.5 megabyte (= about a half-million characters). One night of CCD observation would fill seventy-five floppy disks for storage, which led to the use of magnetic tapes by the thousands. And the laser disk (each one of which can store one thousand megabytes of information), while of course not solving problems of meaning, made it easier for astronomers to enrich (or burden) themselves with more convenient modes of storing the daily accelerating volume of data. Thus, the word "astronomical" has taken on a metaphorical meaning more vivid and more daunting than ever before.

Perhaps as a layman I am not sufficiently grateful for the new treasures of data that the modern technology of discovery has brought into being. Every new byte is another chip of raw material for some scientist's improved description of what the universe really is, some new speculation of how it came into being, and how it may end. But even the most arcane scientific notions, however garbled, penetrate somehow to conscientious literate laymen, among whom I count myself. If we cannot grasp the meanings of Einstein's theories of special and general relativity, or the implications of quantum mechanics, we still can have some general impression of how and where modern discoverers are pointing.

Some obvious characteristics of the modern realms of discovery are perhaps more striking and affecting to a layman than to the scientist who lives among them. While space scientists and cosmologists may not yet have succeeded in producing a satisfactory Grand Unified Theory (GUT), they have, at least in the eye of the lay spectator, actually produced a universe of Grand Unified Data—expanding at an ever-accelerating rate. As never before, space scientists have brought all the cosmic questions together—questions of the very small and the very large, questions of first-time beginnings and final ends, the relations of present phenomena to the whole past and the whole future. They have turned astronomy into a historical science, and made physics into cosmology. And with what effect on us, the lay community?

The familiar troubled voice of John Donne (1572?–1631) eloquently complained, in 1611, that the new Copernican notions were "creeping into every man's mind" and "may very well be true."

> And new Philosophy calls all in doubt,
> The Element of fire is quite put out;
> The Sun is lost, and th'earth, and no man's
>   wit
> Can well direct him where to looke for it.
> And freely men confesse that this world's
>   spent,
> When in the Planets, and the Firmament
> They seek so many new; then see that this
> Is crumbled out againe to his Atomies.
> 'Tis all in peeces, all coherence gone;
> All just supply, and all Relation. . . .
> And in these Constellations then arise
> New starres, and old doe vanish from our
>   eyes . . .

If the mere displacing of the earth from the center of the solar system was so disturbing to the thoughtful layman then, what must be the consequence in our time of the discovery that our whole solar system, our whole Milky Way, our whole galaxy, our whole universe is only a negligible peripheral one of countless billions? John Donne was troubled that the old answers were no longer true. But modern science has long since inoculated us against the permanence of all answers.

Perhaps we are no longer merely *Homo sapiens* but rather *Homo ludens*—at play in the fields of the stars. Perhaps we have learned to luxuriate—as Stephen Hawking's little book suggests—in the expanding universe of expanding questions. Perhaps the modern realm of discovery is no longer a realm of answers but only of questions, which we are beginning to feel at home in and enjoy. Perhaps our modern discoverer is not a discoverer at all but rather a quester, in an age of negative discovery, where achievements are measured not in the finality of answers, but in the fertility of questions. So let us enjoy the quest together. As Claude Bernard (1813–1878), the great French physiologist, observed, "Art is I; Science is We."

And we may express our common challenge in an age of negative discovery in familiar words far less elegant than those of John Donne,

> As I was going up the stair
> I met a man who wasn't there.
> He wasn't there again today.
> I wish, I wish, he'd go away.

But he won't go away, and not only that. The little man who isn't there, the little question we never imagined, will be the constant enticing companion of our common quest.

2

The Cultures of Pride and Awe

Much of the world that we enjoy and admire lay outside the discoverer's ken, even when man's discovering energies were at full flood. In our age of overweening pride in man's power over the physical world, reviewing the achievements of man the creator can balance our view of human nature and be an antidote to the contagion of science.

In both the sciences and the arts, Europe's Age of Exploration—from Marco Polo to Magellan—was an era of spectacular achievement. The era astonishes us with its works of discovery and of creation, inspiring our pride and awe. But the usual rituals of the quincentennial year of Columbus's voyage tempt us to a festival only of pride in man's ability to brave the unknown, to increase his knowledge and mastery of the world. Our National Gallery and other great galleries of art exist to show us that such a celebration would recognize only one side of man's adventuring nature. Neither then nor now could man live by science alone. No generation has been more grossly tempted than ours to luxuriate in the pride of scientific power.

Our great museums of art can remind us how disparate, though sometimes complementary, are the culture of discovery and the culture of creation. The discoverer's work is often the prosaic charting and measuring and extrapolating, to define where man has already reached. The exhilaration of his work requires the artist or poet. It took Keats to remind us of the "wild surmise" awakened in

> . . . some watcher of the skies
> When a new planet swims into his ken;
> Or like stout Cortéz, when with eagle eyes
> He stared at the Pacific. . . .
> Silent upon a peak in Darien.

But vast oceans of ignorance, infinite vistas of human creation, were still unknown to Europeans in the Age of Exploration.

Columbus's life and work offered an allegory of the culture of discovery—international, collaborative, and progressive. The Genoese Columbus had sought support from several other sovereigns before he allowed himself to be enlisted by Ferdinand and Isabella. The maps he relied on had their origins in the efforts of Jewish cartographers at least a century before, and of the Alexandrian Ptolemy long before that. His voyages were conspicuous feats of organization and command, holding the crews together and keeping up their morale under threats of mutiny. Columbus relied on the best manuscripts and printed books of his time to impress Isabella's experts. Despite the limits to his information, and the misinformation that made his voyage seem possible, it was the community of scientific knowledge of his time, the accumulating heritage of centuries, that sent him across the ocean.

The other grand voyages of the Age of Exploration were also products of collaboration. They, too, drew on the international community of knowledge and expertise. In 1498 Vasco da Gama might not have succeeded in his voyage around Africa to India, proving the error in the Ptolemaic maps that had made the Indian Ocean into an enclosed sea, had he not been able to enlist an Arab pilot at Malindi to guide his fleet the twenty-three days across the treacherous Arabian sea to Calicut. An unsung godfather and catalyst of all these voyages had been the sedentary

Prince Henry the Navigator of Portugal. Though a reluctant navigator himself, he had marked the adventuring paths for European sailors and cheered them on their way. Henry, too, had found clues for the design of his miraculous "caravels," which rounded Africa, in the Arab "caravos" long used off the Egyptian and Tunisian coasts, and modeled on the ancient fishing vessels of the Greeks. The printing press, which had come to Europe only decades before Columbus's voyage, was an unprecedented fountain for sharing knowledge, spreading information (and misinformation) to people who earlier had been grateful for only a trickle.

Geographic knowledge, a product of discovery, was a precious international currency, coveted by everyone, easily stolen, and valuable to hoard. Anybody's new bit of information about an easy passage or a treacherous shore could be added to anybody else's in the race for gold and glory. The secrecy rigorously enforced on the fruits of discovery must have cost the lives of many an indiscreet sailor. The Portuguese "policy" of secrecy was itself so secret that some have even denied that it existed. On the other hand, recent champions of Portuguese primacy in the American voyages have dared to use the very absence of documentary evidence as evidence that the Portuguese discoveries must have been too valuable to share.

In the long run secrecy could not prevail. For discovery, this realm of science, was by its very nature collaborative and cumulative. Europe's community treasure-house of geographic knowledge from the past was inevitably international. Columbus was a young man of seventeen at the death of Gutenberg in 1468. Now printed books, themselves potent products of this Age of Exploration, made knowledge even more fluid, more mobile, more difficult to confine in national boundaries. And now the barriers of language, multiplied by the change from Latin to the vernaculars of emerging nations, would be more obstructive than rivers and mountains. But these barriers, too, were soon penetrated by the newly flourishing arts of translation. And the vernacular languages became widening currents of exchange.

Despite all obstacles, news of Columbus's first voyage spread speedily across Europe. Columbus's "letter" describing what he thought he had accomplished, first written in Spanish and printed in Barcelona about April 1, 1493, was translated into Latin as *De Insulis Inventis* and published in Rome before the end of that month. Before the end of the year there were three more editions in Rome, and within the next year six different Latin editions were printed in Paris, Basel, and Antwerp. Soon there was a translation into German, and by mid-June 1493 the Latin Letter had been translated into a 68-stanza poem and published in Tuscan, the dialect of Florence. The Aldine Press in Venice and others across Europe prospered by diffusing knowledge.

Discovery was obviously a progressive science. How to add your bits of new knowledge to others' in the never-ending battle against ignorance? In many ways the age of Columbus was an epoch of scientific advance and climax. Cartography, the proto-science for explorers, was making great progress. Ptolemy was still the patron saint of astronomy and geography. But by 1459 the planisphere map made for the king of Portugal by Fra Mauro in his workshop near Venice revised Ptolemy's version, which had shown that the Indian Ocean was inaccessible by water from Europe, and bore the first mention of Japan on a European map. The Waldseemüller world map of 1507 was the first to put the label "America" on the new world, and his new edition of Ptolemy's *Geography* came to be known as the first modern atlas.

In the fifteenth century a whole new way of looking at the earth was coming into being. In place of the legendary and theological maps that had placed Jerusalem at the center, the earth was being measured, and mapmakers were offering their calculations to the aid of navigators. Now the portolano, the pilot book that was a product of newly extensive use of the magnetic compass, aimed to provide accurate maps of limited regions. And portolano charts, which were first designed to help Mediterranean sailors find their way along the surrounding coastlines, began to be made for the west coasts of Europe and of Africa.

The famous Catalan Atlas of 1375, ornate by modern standards, was a monument to the new empirical spirit. Though a quarter century after the return of Niccolò, Maffeo, and Marco Polo, it is the first map to show the informative influence of their travels, and the first to give Europeans a reasonably accurate description of East Asia. Notable for what it omitted, it showed the courage to leave out mythical and conjectural data that had populated maps for the Christian centuries. And in an impressive feat of self-control, the cartographer actually left parts of the earth blank, in the spirit of the harbor-finding portolano charts that gave only information useful for reaching a known destination. Vast regions once embellished by anthropophagi and mythical monsters here remained vacant, waiting to be filled in by the reports of hardheaded sea captains. And now at last geographic spaces were shaped into the sterile geometry of latitude and longitude. Even before 1501, the era of incunabula when printing was still in its cradle, there were seven folio editions of Ptolemy's classic *Geography,* which had finally been translated from the Greek and was continually being revised from the latest travel reports. The rediscovered Ptolemy provided a framework on which geographers could hang the new bits of discovery.

And navigators were continually improving their instruments. The earlier Islamic astrolabes were models for the elegant late-fifteenth-century astrolabes of Martin Bylica and Alphanus Severus, which show us how far the instrument-makers had come from the primitive wooden disk suspended by a ring that was familiar to the ancients. One of the oldest of scientific instruments, the device had been used to observe and chart the heavenly bodies. Now the astrolabe had become an instrument of navigation accurate enough to help mariners find their latitude. In the next centuries it would be displaced by the quadrant and the sextant. In 1484, Martin Behaim was said to be the first to adapt the astrolabe to navigation. He is best remembered for the terrestrial globe he constructed in Nuremberg, which is more notable for its beauty than for its verisimilitude.

In this grand universal enterprise of discovery, all scientists, explorers, and navigators were collaborating willy-nilly, intentionally or unintentionally. Collaboration, while necessary, was both desired and feared. All realized that they were working toward the same end, a more accurate map of the earth. And their efforts bore fruit. European experts knew much more about the world in 1550 than in 1450. The European "discovery" of America not only provided new destinations for civilization. It enlarged and redefined European knowledge of the whole earth. Whatever ills feudalism, chivalry, and the Crusades may have visited on the peoples of the West, the new centuries never failed to bring more accurate maps, and better instruments for making the future maps even more accurate.

Still, inherited "facts" had a dignity and a prestige that made them hard to displace. They had become the basis not only of myth and lore but of commercial hopes and political ambitions. Displacing the old geographic knowledge by the new was always painful, and often resisted. Columbus found it hard to doubt that what he saw on the shores of the Caribbean was the Terrestrial Paradise. When Vespucci showed these figments of ancient desire to be unimagined real continents, he shocked learned Europeans, but he nourished pride in the advances of their "modern" science. Reports of pagan temple sacrifices and cannibal feasts, documented by sacrificial knives brought back, impressed Europeans with their own superiority over the heathen. The greatest discovery of an age of discoveries was to realize how little of the earth was known to Europe. Never before had such vast areas of ignorance been so suddenly unveiled.

Discoverers everywhere focused their vision on the same object—the physical, sensible earth that all shared. They brought the unknown down to earth. All were marching in the same direction. Ptolemy advanced along the lines marked by Aristotle, Vespucci on the lines marked by Ptolemy. Discovery reinforced faith in human collaboration and human progress. And it sparked the sense of being born again in a Europe-wide Renaissance.

In this brilliant Age of Exploration, European man flexed his scientific muscles. When had there been more reason for pride in what man could do? Or in his capacity to discover new areas of his ignorance? This age, "Circa 1492," was a tonic for man's belief in his power to master wind and wave, to find and then conquer terra incognita.

A steady forward march against the unknown is only one sort of human effort. What our art galleries celebrate is the culture of creation. The happy coincidence that in Europe the epoch-making Age of Exploration was also an epoch-making Age of Creation gives us now the dramatic opportunity to compare the two cultures. Renaissance belief in the inspired unique creator elevated the painter, equipped with a newly rediscovered science of perspective, from craftsman to artist. No longer paid by the hour like other skilled laborers, he began to be liberated from guild traditions. And now the artist himself was being sought after by kings and popes, who left him free to conceive and execute his personal vision. We must not allow glib attacks on the philistinism of scientists to blind us to the real gulf between the two cultures. The whole world of the arts, mostly still unknown to Europeans in the age of Columbus, can remind us of the limits of the pride-nourishing culture of discovery.

Peoples competing and collaborating in the search for knowledge are inevitably converging. Discovery is what men everywhere have found on our same earth. But creation is what men have added to the world. Its hallmark is autonomy, the freedom to make the new. While there are, of course, traditions and styles and schools in the arts, every act of creation is a kind of personal declaration of independence. Which makes the story of art infinitely more confused and confusing than the story of science. The culture of creation comprises countless communities of artists, each daring to be a community of one. The diversity, the diffuseness, the chaos is what makes representative works of art.

In the age of Columbus, artists in Portugal, Spain, Genoa, and Venice give us glimpses of Europe's variegated culture of creation. And how disparate were the works of artists on the other side of the world! In Japan the delicate brushwork of Sesshu (1419–1506) and the masks and ceramics of the prolific Muromachi era, in China the monumental paintings of the Ming imperial palaces, and in India and Tibet sculptures of the flourishing Buddhist traditions. These many worlds of the arts show us a kaleidoscope of visions and of styles—African bronzes and ivories, Brazilian featherwork, Mississippian stone effigies, Aztec codices, Costa Rican and Colombian gold jewelry.

If we are puzzled and startled by this miscellany, still mostly hidden from Columbus's European contemporaries, it is because we have begun to see the distinctiveness of the culture of discovery and the culture of creation. So we can correct the myopic vision of our discovery pride. We become aware of the limits of the kinds of fulfillment that dominate the consciousness in an age of science. While the culture of discovery was an invisible community forged in the spirit of quest and focused on the same object, an earth to be mastered and mapped, winds and ocean currents to be harnessed, accumulating and sharing fragments from everywhere, the culture of creation was a host of countless independents. Their only limits were their inherited styles and materials. Each was aiming at a personal target. These heterogeneous and chaotic worlds, instead of nourishing our pride in a generalized mankind, should inspire our awe at the infinite capacities of atomic individuals. We see an astonishing, even bewildering, array. We must be struck by the diffuseness and disconnectedness of man's efforts in different places to express himself. The subtle masks of Noh players contrast spectacularly with the monumental palace paintings of Ming artists and the massive rotundity of Aztec sculpture. It is folly to try to put them in a line. Not progress, surely, but endless variety! In this fertile chaos we see individual artists, and mankind, moving infinitely in all directions. We see every artist inventing an artist. As uncanny as the inevitable collaboration of discoverers is the uncanny uniqueness of creators.

Sometimes, of course, traditions converge or compete, and often artists learn from other artists, just as the Japanese painter Sesshu learned from his life among the artists of Ming China, or as Dürer learned from Italian painters in Venice. Then each does much more than translate. He transforms these predecessors.

While discoverers are marching or trying to march to the same tune, the world of creators tells us no such simple story. Each is his own compass, not finding but making his directions. How random and diffuse were man's efforts to create in an era when, more effectively than ever before, leaders of Western Europe were competing for the common currency of discovery! Creations are the strange fruit of diverging imaginations. Vasco da Gama might not have reached India without that Arab navigator. But there was no Arab apprentice or mentor in Leonardo da Vinci's studio. The earlier maps were displaced by the later, and Columbus's compass itself was an improved model. His voyage was promptly excelled by later navigators. So, too, the anatomy and physics of da Vinci and Dürer would be displaced. But Leonardo's *Ginevra de' Benci* and Dürer's *Knight, Death and the Devil* would never become obsolete. The designs of Ming China and Inca stonework remain treasured originals. Textbooks can arrange maps in a clear line of progress, from Ptolemy and T-O medieval versions, advancing through Fra Mauro's planisphere, Waldseemüller's world, and Battista Agnese's portolano world atlas—and endlessly on into the future.

In the culture of creation there is no correct or incorrect, and in the long run no progress. Works of art reveal no linear direction but experiments radiating in all directions. While the post-Columbian maps of the world make their predecessors obsolete, works of art are always additive. They provide the pleasures of novelty and addition without pains of subtraction. Pre-Columbian arts only gain from modern comparisons.

The two cultures differ too in the roles they assign to the individual. Oddly enough, though discovery is the arena of collaboration, it offers its historic prizes for individual priority. There is something decisive and exclusive about every first discoverer. Although great discoveries, including Columbus's, are a team product, it is somehow always *the* "discoverer" who gets the credit. Columbus has no peer. While cities and nations are named after him, historians still debate the Portuguese claims, some demand the laurels for Leif Eriksson or an Irish Saint Brendan. The laurels that go to the one are lost to all the others. Discovery seems to be a history of firsts.

But the culture of creation offers no simple superlatives or absolutes. While the arts celebrate the unique and the original, the uniqueness of the artist, even the greatest, is usually incremental. The individual differences between the works of Piero della Francesca and Leonardo da Vinci are minute, but they add up to reveal the works of different artists. Their works can easily be distinguished, and the pleasures of the art historian come from the irrelevance of "firsts" and "bests." We can speak of the style or "school" of a da Vinci or a Dürer that can diminish the value of a work claimed for the master. But we do not speak of the "school" of Copernicus, Columbus, or Magellan. The culture of creation is full of minor variants and near misses, but the culture of discovery insists on naming the winner of first prize. The scene of discoverers, then, is dominated by a star system. Each new idol displaces idols of the last generation and is destined to be displaced in turn. Yet hero-artists like da Vinci and Dürer never lose their starring role.

· · ·

The great civilizations produce their own special triumphs of both discovery and creation. And each offers us its own distinctive large area of overlap. Technology, bastard offspring of the two cultures, uses the fruits of past discoveries for surprising future creations. And technology can mislead us into the illusion that there is progress in art and that somehow the findings of science can be made immortal, immune to displacement. The portable, durable, and accessible works of craftsmen put their stamp on our popular notions of other civilizations. We are impressed by the distinctive skills of Flemish weavers, Portuguese silversmiths, Spanish ceramicists, Turkish swordsmiths, and Colombian jewelers, by the makers of Chinese lacquer and Korean porcelain. Every triumph of craftsmen has been made possible by earlier findings of the properties of wool, silver, jade, bronze, steel, or glass. The achievements of sculptors and painters become possible by discovering the special qualities of marble, of tempera and oil. The cultures of creation and of discovery meet in a fertile limbo.

Europe's Age of Exploration was an era of awesome achievements in the three hybrid arts of cartography, perspective, and anatomy. In these years European cartography probably made more progress than in the millennium before. Even after explorers on the real earth ceased to be satisfied by the theological symmetries and mythological embellishments on their maps, they still expected their maps to be decorative objects. Accustomed as we are to the antiseptic schematic newspaper maps of our time, we can especially enjoy the elegance of an Islamic celestial globe of 1275 or the whimsies of camels and elephants and giraffes, of sultans and emperors, that still adorn the Catalan Atlas of 1375, and the many-handed monsters and monstrosities of the Nuremberg Chronicle of 1493. We see science translated onto a tapestry of the mechanism of the universe or of the astronomer's visions. The navigator's instruments, his globe and astrolabe attain a filigreed elegance to equal that of the silver for communion or for the royal table.

In the Age of Exploration, "perspective," a medieval synonym for the science of sight or optics, became a name for a rediscovered ancient art. With this came epochal progress in man's capacity to capture space on paper or on canvas, to translate the three-dimensional world into persuasive two dimensions. We can see the fruits of this rediscovery in the studies of Uccello, the treatise and works of Piero della Francesca, and delightfully idealized plans for Italian cities. Dürer himself took the trouble to show us how a draftsman could use the new perspective device. The technique that Giotto had applied by rule of thumb became a science in the hands of da Vinci or Dürer.

"Anatomy," originally a name simply for dissection or cutting up, in the Age of Exploration was beginning to mean the science of bodily structure. Da Vinci and Dürer, both pioneers of anatomy, made it the ally and handmaiden of their painting and sculpture. Leonardo da Vinci used what he had learned at the dissecting table (seen in his drawings of sections of a human head and of the urogenital system of a woman) while the mathematically minded Dürer constructed his *Adam and Eve* with a compass and ruler. Artists felt new need for the science of anatomy when they made nudes a focus of their Renaissance vision. In the history of science and of art, rarely have the talents for both kinds of human fulfillment been so brilliantly embodied in the same artist, as we see in Leonardo da Vinci and Albrecht Dürer.

In our age of triumphant science, we are inordinately proud of the progressive powers of discovery. Knowledge is still the most precious international currency. The triumphs of technology, too, still bring the world together in the marketplace and on the battlefield. Both science and technology, but especially technology, assimilate the ways of life of people everywhere. Photography, television, the airplane, and the computer erase time and space.

So today we are more than ever in need of the impulse of the arts for the variety of creation. Salesmen assure us of the pro-

gressive improvements in every new model, every latest "generation" of their devices. Research and development laboratories
confidently and deliberately chart the course of the future. Refugees from the extrapolations of statistics and the certitudes of
advertising, we must welcome the wonderfully random unpredictable arts.

Here we can take ourselves off the speedy tracks of progress
and enjoy the fertile chaos of the arts. Just as the Europeans of
the Age of Exploration were ignorant of the creations of most of
the world in their time, so our confident lines of discovery can
give us no hint of the spectrums of creation. The worldwide
creations unknown to Europeans in one of the great ages of
European exploration can remind us of the still-vast continents
of our own ignorance. While knowledge is a moving target and
old maps are discarded for new, works of art hold their place
with richly iridescent afterlives. As every generation and every
great scientist displaces the works of predecessors, the stature of
a scientific work is measured by how many earlier works it
makes obsolete. But the artists only add. They are the re-creators
of the world. Later artists help us discover the earlier, just as
they will acquire new interest from the works of artists still unborn. While artists can inspire our awe, they can make us wary
of the conceit, bred by all ages of discovery, including our own,
that by mastering more of the world we can ever encompass the
mysterious vagaries of the human spirit, of man the creator.

3

An Odd Couple:
Discoverers and Inventors

Man, we are told, is the inventing animal. He is also the discovering animal. Through most of history these two features of human nature have seemed quite separate. Discovery has been everybody's everyday experience. We live and learn—which means we constantly discover. But inventions have been rare and far between.

World discoverers have advanced inch by inch, gradually across deserts, slowly down the coasts of Africa, island by island across the Pacific. Every age adds its own discoveries to the legacy handed down by its grandfathers. While history has been punctuated by the melodrama of great discoveries—of the earth's path around the sun, of passageways around the world, of the constellations within the atom—the processes of discovery have been unceasing and incremental. Seldom has anything once discovered—the shape of a continent, the source of a river, the anatomy of the atom—ever been forgotten or successfully concealed.

But few ages have seen great world-transforming inventions. The incremental inventions that were being made throughout history have left few records. Speech and language and writing, the wheel and the sail, the stirrup and the plow, which marked epochs in the rise of civilization, were usually invented anonymously over ill-defined millennia.

When I selected great discoverers in Western civilization for my book *The Discoverers,* I had to make invidious choices. For every little advance along a risky, half-known path, every mountain first climbed, river sources found, desert crossed or island mapped has enlarged human life and opportunities. Yet it was possible to tell the story of great Western waves of discovery with only occasional mention of the world-changing inventions. This reminded me of the remarkable separation of discoverers from inventors during most of history. We all know the names of the great discoverers—from Democritus and Aristotle to Copernicus, Galileo, Columbus, Pasteur, and Einstein. But only the historian of technology can name the great inventors before recent times.

Time—the primordial dimension of history—was charted and measured by the instruments of anonymous inventors. The technology for measuring time—the water clock, the sundial, the pendulum, the mechanical clock, and the sailors' instruments for taking bearings by the sun and the stars—made possible the epochal discoveries of Columbus, Copernicus, and Galileo. But these elementary time-measuring devices were invented and perfected over centuries. Often they were communal achievements. People agreed on the definitions of the sundial, recognized the chiming of the clock on the square or the bell in the church tower, and shared the experiences of sailors using cross-staff and astronomical tables to help refine latitude. Those who defined the instruments of timekeeping—Christiaan Huygens, William Clement, Robert Hooke, and John Harrison among others—do not enter our history books until recent centuries. Meanwhile, whole communities had come to share the accumulating benefits of the improving technologies of time measurement—in the promptness of private and public meetings, in the regularity of church worship, in the shared fruits of adventuring seafarers and scrupulous cartographers. We cannot know whom to thank for these conveniences.

The classic chronicle of discovery is anything but anonymous.

On the contrary, it is intensely, even intimately, personal. Columbus's achievement was a work of salesmanship, courage, expertise, knowledge of wind and current, organizational ability, and stick-to-itiveness. He did have a compass and could find his bearings by ancient methods. But his was a personal, not a technological, triumph. Nobody before him had just the qualities, or found quite the opportunity, to do it.

To make sense of the story of the great discoverers, then, I needed to chronicle only a few crucial inventions. These included the clock, the compass, the printing press, the telescope, and the microscope. The contrast, too, between where the great discoverers and the great inventors commonly did their work is quite striking. Both were a varied and unpredictable lot. But we can say that the great discoverers—openers of vistas—more often than not worked in the open air. Of course among discoverers too there were conspicuous exceptions—the Galens and Harveys. Still, generally speaking, discoverers were darers—who rode the oceans, climbed the mountains, peered into the heavens. Even the great works of discovering antiquity were risky. They required digging amid suspicious inhabitants in the ruins of Mycenae and Troy, in the tomb of Tutankhamun or the wind-swept deserts of Mesopotamia.

Inventors, in sharp contrast, were commonly artisans. Their habitat was the stuffy workshop, where they forged axles, cut cogs on wheels, polished lenses and mirrors. While more often than not the discoverer had his eyes set on a distant horizon of space or time, the inventor commonly was myopic. He focused sharply, measured closely, so he could fit all the parts together. The inventor shaped what he held in his hand. The weakness of the one was far-sight, overlooking nearby obstacles, and of the other was near-sight, ignoring the long vistas.

Until modern times, these were two worlds with hopes and visions of quite different dimensions. The great discoverer, the Columbus, needed the sponsorship of sovereigns to finance expeditions, to defend voyages and finds against unknown savages

and unfriendly rivals. The great inventor was apt to be an artisan working securely within his guild.

An unsung revolution, more basic even than the historians' Industrial Revolution, has united these two worlds. In modern
times, as never before, adventurer and artisan have been assimilated into a single community of questing mankind. Western
progress since the eighteenth century has dramatically mixed
and unified their roles. Modern discoverer and modern inventor
have been drawn together by forces beyond their control in an
undeclared, sometimes involuntary, partnership. Of course the
restless personalities vary as much as ever. But now inventors
have been taken out into the open air—to the deep ocean bottom and the oxygen-rare mountaintops. At the same time discoverers have walked into the wilderness of the laboratory.

This new unlimited partnership can be dated from about the
beginning of the eighteenth century. "Scientists," a new word,
signaled the new partnership. Surprisingly, its first recorded use
did not come until 1840. "We need very much a name," said the
brilliant English philosopher-mathematician William Whewell
(1794–1866), "to describe a cultivator of science in general. I
should incline to call him a Scientist." About the same time the
realm of the artisan was being transformed, and the word "artist" came into use to describe "one who practices a manual art in
which there is much room for display of taste; one who makes
his craft a 'fine art.' " When the inventor-craftsman was natural-
ized into the realms of science, his aesthetic role was taken from
him to be added to the artisans in the fine arts. A prophetic
writer in *Blackwood's Magazine* in 1840 explained, "Leonardo
was mentally a seeker after truth—a scientist; Correggio was an
assertor of truth—an artist."

The modern community of the "cultivator of science in general" was even more novel and more revolutionary than Whewell imagined. This new age might have been christened the age
of invention, just as its predecessor in the fifteenth century was

the age of discovery. But it would have been misleading, by perpetuating the disappearing distinction.

The new era signaled an unprecedented symbiosis. Of the few earlier world-transforming inventions, one in particular symbolized and declared the new unity of artisans and knowledge seekers. This was, of course, the new art of printing. Gutenberg and his main partner, Fust, who were only goldsmiths, managed to devise "the art preservative of all the arts." Printing, a humble invention, became the whole world's vehicle of discovery. Every age now had the power to inherit the whole world's legacy of discoveries—and leave its own to all later times. What better symbol than printing for the modern collaboration of inventors and discoverers? Succeeding centuries would cement this collaboration.

The modern inventors' transformations of experience were usually by-products. These unintended, outreaching, everyone-touching consequences were possible because inventors took possession of three new areas. They assumed at least three new roles. They became devisers of new materials. They became makers of new sources of energy. And they crafted new instruments for sharing experience.

The prosaic innovations in mining and metallurgy during the Industrial Revolution deserve far more dignity than historians usually give them. For millennia alchemists had tried to turn base metals into gold. But the new ways of mining and of making iron more versatile—and then of compounding iron into steel—were worth many gold mines. Iron and steel would make possible the devices that mined the coal to produce more iron and steel. And these became the skeletons for the machines of mass production. Later the myriad new plastics would multiply all these possibilities a thousandfold. The innovators faced the troublesome but exhilarating problem of inventing names— from Bakelite to nylon—for materials that God had never created.

The novelty of the steam engine was less in its new power than in the outlandish idea that man could make and harness new kinds of power. A melodramatic symbol—of the new unity of discovery and invention, of the new outdoor habitat of the inventor, and of the sharing of risks between inventor and discoverer—was Benjamin Franklin with his electrical kite and his lightning rod. In a single dangerous experiment he identified a new force. He would prove too that the Old World separations into kinds of electrical magnetism were an illusion. At once he provided a new device for the protection, propulsion, and illumination of mankind. The bizarre possibility of new kinds of energy became less bizarre with the elaboration of electrical power and the invention of the internal combustion engine.

Most outlandish of all was the discovery that the power in the "unbreakable" atom could move factories, transform warfare, unbalance the balances of power among nations, and might even shatter the planet. The daily news dramatized the obsolescence of old distinctions between artisan and adventurer. The world had become an open-air laboratory, and the scientist's workshop had become a jungle of discovery. It was not easy to calculate or control the by-products of the new discoverer-inventor partnerships. Would the new forces of energy—mechanical, chemical, nuclear—produce new forms of waste? Where to put them? Or perhaps try to invent new uses for them?

Another gargantuan and curious new power distinguished the new-age inventions. They no longer merely increased man's capacity to make or improve familiar products—to dig, and cut, and shape, and move, and build, and destroy. They created a strange new set of tasks, from novel ways to share experience. Photography and electronics captured and diffused the visual image, the heard voice, the sensations of moving and of being encompassed. New devices assimilated places and times, recaptured the moving images of the dead, the invisible, and the remote. The inventor had unwittingly become an impresario, playing the role of public discoverer with his camera, telephone, phonograph, radio, motion-picture camera, projector, television set, or VCR. He had become an opener and amplifier of worlds for the millions.

New technologies were doing for all experience what printing did for knowledge. Steam transportation moved commodities and the people who made them across oceans. Electricity enlarged the day and illuminated the night. Steam power eased the production of electricity, and electronics carried information, ideas, and images everywhere.

The world became a discovering community. The discoverer in a space capsule en route to the moon came into everybody's living room. Timid stay-at-homes shared the dangerous moments. A whole nation could feel the suspense, the hope, and the terror of the great ventures, at the moment of triumph—landing on the moon—or of tragedy—the explosion of the *Challenger*. Would the modern Ulysses and Columbuses and Magellans still be heroes? We all were there!

The new partnership of the search to know—discovery—and the passion to innovate—invention—made it newly impossible to prophesy impossibilities. We were losing our capacity for surprise. Some new light material, some new propellant, and some new airplane design had broken the sound barrier! After the moon there was Mars, and after Mars . . . ? Was there any limit to the capacity of future "generations" of computers? In recent history had not the most expert predictors of impossibility (like Rutherford on the atom) been proven wrong? Every invention widened vistas and so multiplied opportunities for the "cultivator of science in general." Naysayers found their scripts destroyed. Cassandras were obsolete. One after another, impossible discoveries (the sensation of walking weightless on the moon) were accomplished by impossible inventions (computer technology). The word "impossible," which sententious moralists from Epictetus to William Ernest Henley and Rudyard Kipling had tried in vain to banish from the young man's lexicon, lost its meaning in the new community of inventors and discoverers. Dared man at long last say, "I am the master of my fate"?

Every day invention was serving discovery in new ways. Glass display windows enticed consumers with new products. Special glass for scientific instruments, which survived the highest and the lowest temperatures, sharpened vision in the laboratory. Photography with novel sensitivities captured and diffused images of what was once invisible. Electronic technology and computers multiplied miracles of everyday discovery. Atomic energy and lasers catapulted into the unimagined.

This exhilarating collaboration has brought new temptations, without destroying the old. Discoverers continue to be menaced by the illusion of knowledge. Inventors continue to be menaced by the terminal fallacy, the illusion that a final improvement has been made.

The framers of our federal Constitution prophetically glimpsed this partnership when it was just beginning. They gave to Congress (Article I, Section 8) the power by laws of patent and copyright: "To promote the Progress of Science [discovery] and useful Arts [invention]." It was this emerging community of the "cultivators of science in general" for whom our twentieth century would create new institutions. Universities became fertile centers. "Research and Development" (1923) entered our language as businesses risked billions on the new partnership. An odd couple—the courageous heroic Ulysses and the dogged prosaic Edison—were cemented in a partnership unlikely ever to be dissolved.

II

TRIALS OF CONSCIENCE

O conscience, into what abyss of fears
And horrors hast thou driven me; out of which
I find no way, from deep to deeper plung'd!

—John Milton, *Paradise Lost*

4

The Writer as Conscience of the World

"Conscience and Cowardice," Oscar Wilde emended Shakespeare, "are really the same things. Conscience is the trade-name of the firm." Or, as H. L. Mencken put it, conscience is "the inner voice that warns us that someone may be looking." No word in our language is richer in ironic ambiguities. Living in Washington, D.C., I find new reasons every day to be wary of people who are solicitous of other people's consciences.

The word "conscience" itself implies the problems and opportunities of the writer as a divided self, someone who speaks *for* himself and *to* the world. We writers live in the limbo between expression and communication. And we do not need theology or metaphysics to remind us that as writers we cannot avoid the effort, or the temptation, to serve two masters—ourselves, what is within us, and our readers, our conjectural clients outside. Western literature offers us countless different ways in which authors have dealt with this divided self. I will provide only a sample from some of my favorite writers that may suggest the perils that beset writers who pretend to be the world's arbiters.

The doubleness—the ambivalence—in the very idea of conscience is rooted in its etymology. The English "conscience" is derived from the Latin *conscientia,* which means "joint knowledge." The Greek synonym *syneidesis* (also "joint knowledge") was defined to mean a sense of "oughtness," a comparative eval-

uation of ways of conduct and a censuring of the self for choos-
ing the wrong way. From Cicero, the word is variously translated as "conscience" or "consciousness," a pregnant ambiguity
that survives also in the French word *conscience*. In English the
word "conscience" has lately taken on the primary meaning of
"the faculty within us that decides on the moral quality of our
thoughts, words, acts." Dr. Johnson marked the modern path of
the word in his *Dictionary*. "Conscience . . . 1. The knowledge
or faculty by which we judge of the goodness or wickedness of
ourselves." But the taint of ambiguity remains, with his closely
following senses of "2. Justice," and "3. Consciousness."

I will offer three examples of ways of defining conscience
prominently reflected in Western literature. These are: the Divine Conscience, the Public Conscience, and the Personal Conscience.

Perhaps most inhibiting to the writer is the most ancient way:
the Divine Conscience, whose spokesmen were the prophets.
Their very name—"prophets"—asserted that they spoke for another, that other being God. Biblical prototypes are Isaiah and
Jeremiah. Among Western writers in this genre none is more
effective than Saint Augustine of Hippo (354–430), whose
major works, his *Confessions* and *The City of God,* illustrate
brilliantly the inward and outward directions of the writer
speaking for the world. His *Confessions* brings readers along the
writer's path to the one true God and the Savior, and *The City of
God* fits recent events and history into a Christian destiny for all
mankind. The inward and outward paths of the Divine Conscience that Saint Augustine traced were pursued, widened, and
explored by Western Christianity in the next centuries.

"Confession," the acknowledgment of sin, of the violation of
the duties of conscience, has, of course, become an institution
and played an important role in both Judaism and Christianity.
Old Testament prophets tried to awaken people to a sense of
their sin, and an acknowledgment of their guilt, personal and

collective. The Day of Atonement has continued among modern Jews to have an uncanny redolence even for those whose other Jewish associations have been diluted or dissolved. Confession became a Roman Catholic institution after the Fourth Lateran Council in 1215 and obliged all Catholics to make at least one confession a year.

In the Middle Ages, this institution flourished as the Tribunal of Conscience, with confession an essential part. And it produced a whole body of literature in which writers set themselves up as judges of other people's consciences by prescribing and exploring the proper application of general moral principles to everyday situations. It was simply the "case method" (now familiar in American legal education) applied to morality.

Because it was concerned with applying rules to particular cases (in Latin, *casus,* for case, event, or occurrence), the literature and its mode of thinking came to be called "casuistry." A classic example was Saint Augustine's work "On Lying," in which he posed the question (later analyzed by Kant) "Should you lie to conceal an innocent person from persecution?" This literature of scruples was found not only among Christians but also among Jewish compilers of the Talmud and Muslim commentators on the Koran. Because of the adeptness of Jesuits at this kind of reasoning, the exaggeration of fine distinctions came to be called "Jesuitical." By the eighteenth century, "casuistry" in English had become a synonym for specious reasoning, or evasive ways of dealing with difficult cases of duty. One wit called it "the art of quibbling with God."

The Protestant Reformation, obsessed with Personal Conscience, abandoned the "tribunal of conscience" and the priestly confessional. But a Protestant literature of Cases of Conscience flourished, as ministers arrogated an authority over the private conscience not dissimilar to that of the Roman Catholic priest in the confessional. Colonial New England saw Cases of Conscience by the dozens, dealing conclusively with the trivial or the cosmic. For example, Solomon Stoddard's *Answers to Some*

Cases of Conscience Respecting the Country (Boston, 1722), having asked "Whether it is Lawful [for men] to wear long hair?" persuasively condemns the practice as "a great Burden and Cumber . . . Effeminacy, and a vast Expence." Turning to graver questions, Stoddard asks, "Did we any wrong to the Indians in Buying their Land at a small Price?" And he salves the New England conscience by reminding his readers that "God granted the earth for men to subdue," then that "The Indians made no use of it, but for hunting," and "had it continued in their hands, it would have been of little value."

As the market for books widened in the centuries after Gutenberg, as literacy spread, and as new institutions and new technologies of printing and publishing reached out, the word "prophet" took on a new meaning and an interesting new ambiguity. The writer became a divided self in a new sense. The "other" for whom the writer-prophet spoke was no longer God, but His modern stand-in, the Public. Of course, demagoguery is not entirely a modern invention. But the familiar *Vox populi, vox dei,* the axiom of modern best-selling authors, appears long before our modern era of liberalism, representative government, and the printed book. Some attribute its first use to Alcuin (735–804), about the year 800. Charlemagne's energetic assistant at the court of the Franks (781), Alcuin was leader of the Carolingian Renaissance, and he is credited with introducing the standards of Anglo-Saxon humanism to Western Europe. He revised the liturgy and introduced the Irish-Northumbrian custom of singing the Creed.

Still, the notion of a "reading public" is emphatically modern. The first recorded use of the expression "the reading public," according to the *Oxford English Dictionary,* was by Samuel Taylor Coleridge (1772–1834) in 1817. By mid-century (1843), John Ruskin (1819–1900) could observe that "there is a separate public for every picture, and for every book."

Now secular pundits, succeeding the divine prophets and casuists, acquired an awesome popularity. They were prophets of the Public Conscience. Their texts were secular scriptures—state papers, vital statistics, chronicles of poverty and disease, records of the slave trade, tales of the oppression of women and the abuse of children, miseries of factory workers, etc. These again were Cases of Conscience but bore sensational labels in pamphlets, newspapers, magazines, and journals of uplift and philanthropy. The popular literary form was no longer theological or philosophical but simply narrative, vividly located in time and place, in close touch with popular sentiments, hopes, outrages, and aspirations. Harriet Beecher Stowe's *Uncle Tom's Cabin* (1852), the most familiar American example, sold some three hundred thousand copies in its first year.

The novel had now become the modern literary form for casuistry—for applying the society's moral professions to particular cases. The brilliantly successful prophet of the Public Conscience was, of course, Charles Dickens (1812–1870). He prospered by helping the society judge its institutions against the pretensions of individuals and moral credos. There was hardly an institution of Victorian England or nineteenth-century America—schools, criminal laws, lawyers, priests and philanthropists, prisons and poorhouses, to mention only a few—that did not come under his conscientious scrutiny. If the weakness of the theological casuist was legalism, sophism, quibbling, and unctuousness, the novelist-casuist had some opposite temptations. He stirred his readers by sentimentality and melodrama. His risks were not literalism and pedantry but oversimplification and caricature.

The "serial" novel, in which Dickens was an innovator, made it convenient, prudent, and profitable for the novelist to consult the Public Conscience—or consciousness—as he went along. As each 32-page installment of *The Pickwick Papers* (1836–37) appeared in green paper covers on the last day of the month for one shilling, Dickens could have the reassurance of the marketplace that he was giving the public what they wanted. And if feedback showed him that the story did not suit them, he could try to oblige in the next installment. Dickens called this the novelists' "Periodical paragraph disease." "Other writers," Dickens himself explained in his original preface to *Nicholas Nickleby* (1839), "submit their sentiments to their readers, with the reserve and circumspection of him who has had little time to prepare for a public appearance. . . . But the periodical essayist commits to his readers the feelings of the day, in the language which those feelings have prompted."

Dickens was wonderfully sensitive to this Public Conscience-Consciousness. When the first four serial numbers of *Martin Chuzzlewit* (1843-44) appeared, they did not sell well—only some 20,000 for each number compared to the 50,000 for *Pickwick* and *Nicholas Nickleby* and 100,000 for *The Old Curiosity Shop*. After conferring with his publishers, Chapman and Hall, and his intimate friend John Forster, he decided to profit from the lesson of the spectacular sales of his *American Notes* the year before. He then sent the hero, Martin Chuzzlewit, to America so he could embroider on the more appealing outrageous generalizations in his *American Notes*. Unfortunately, the sales did not respond as he had hoped. Still the product, according to Dickens, was "in a hundred points immeasurably the best" work he had yet written. It was Dickens's boast that the rise of literacy and a widened reading public meant that "the people have set literature free" from the shame of the purchased dedication and servile patronage. But his own career dramatized the literary perils as well as the remunerative opportunities of the newly public "Tribunal of Conscience."

By an ironic twist in the history of Western literature, in this very age of unprecedented temptations to literary populism, an age of the sovereign and increasingly demanding public, there developed a fertile new sense of Personal Conscience. The private consciousness took on a new life and became a wondrous new literary resource. In a modern transformation, conscience, an ancient laboratory of theological hairsplitting and a modern arena of ephemeral public taste, became inward, experimental, and biographical. I have sketched this modern Western creation of the self in Book III of *The Creators*.

This surprising modern adventure in self-scrutiny, this terra incognita of the private world, was signaled in the brilliant writing of Michel de Montaigne (1533–1592). He felt that the self was the only proper judge of the self, yet paradoxically made a literature of these self-judgments. Montaigne's novel device, of course, was the "essay," a name he introduced in what he called "an honest book . . . a private and domestic one." Disparaging the subject matter—"myself"—he warned the reader that "there is no reason why you should waste your leisure on so frivolous and unrewarding a subject." What he offered is much like what earlier Christians would have called "casuistry," the testing of general moral propositions by applying them to specific cases. But in this modern casuistry, Montaigne, and many others after him, would draw cases from their own lives. Montaigne judged the whole man in himself, the microcosm of human nature, with such questions as "That our actions should be judged by our intentions" or "That one man's profit is another's loss."

In his chapter "On Repentance," Montaigne explained:

> Others shape the man; I portray him, and offer to the view one in particular, who is ill-shaped enough, and whom, could I refashion him, I should certainly make very different from whom he is. But there is no chance of that. . . . Moral philosophy, as a whole, can be just as well applied to a common and private existence as to one of richer stuff. Every man carries in himself the complete pattern of human nature.
>
> Authors communicate with the world in some special and peculiar capacity; I am the first to do so with my whole being, as Michel de Montaigne, not as a grammarian, a poet, or a lawyer. If people complain that I speak too much of myself, I complain that they do not think of themselves at all.

And he warned against allowing others to judge oneself:

None but you know whether you are cruel and cowardly, or loyal and dutiful. Others have no vision of you, but judge of you by uncertain conjectures; they see not so much your nature as your artifices. Do not rely on their opinion, therefore; rely on your own. [And from Cicero] "You must use your own judgment about yourself. The inner conscience of virtue and vice exercises a great influence; take that away, and all is in ruins."

There is no man who, if he listens to himself, does not discover within him an individual principle, a ruling principle. . . . [Translated by J. M. Cohen]

This shift of conscience inward—from external rules of divine or public origin toward a personal voice—marked a much wider shift, not merely in morals but in all philosophy and epistemology.

Descartes (1596–1650), often considered "the founder of modern philosophy," was the first to base philosophy on consciousness and to sketch a philosophical method wholly within the limits of consciousness. This basic idea has become familiar in his *Cogito ergo sum*. "What is it that I am?" asked Descartes. "A thinking thing. What is a thinking thing? It is a thing that doubts, understands, affirms, denies, wills, abstains from willing, that also can be aware of images and sensations." Some currents of modern materialism also led to belief in a personal conscience. Thomas Jefferson, who was not a particularly introspective person, was ready to advise his young friend Peter Carr on the "natural history" of the moral faculty (from Paris, 1787). It was a waste of time, he said, to attend lectures on moral philosophy. The Creator "would have been a pitiful bungler, if he had made the rules of our moral conduct a matter of science." Nor was it necessary, for He chose a simpler way, Jefferson explained:

Man was destined for society. His morality, therefore, was to be formed to this object. He was endowed with a sense of right and wrong, merely relative to this. This sense is as much a part of his nature, as the sense of hearing, seeing, feeling; it is the true foundation of morality, and not the . . . truth, etc., as fanciful writers have imagined. The moral sense of conscience is as much a part of man as his leg or arm. It is given to all human beings in a stronger or weaker degree. . . . It may be strengthened by exercise, as may any particular limb of the body.

For writers more philosophically inclined than Jefferson, when the medieval "tribunal of conscience" was transformed inward into a personal faculty, it became a newly fertile literary resource. Fallibility and the idea of the infinite were at the heart of Descartes's concerns and made his troubled conscience central to his philosophy. Blaise Pascal (1623–1662), too, proceeded down this path—with *Les Provinciales* (1656–57) targeting Jesuitical casuistry and his *Pensées* (1670), of fragmentary eloquence. And Pascal became an apostle of belief. "We have an incapacity for proving anything," he observed, "which no amount of dogmatism can overcome. We have an idea of truth which no amount of skepticism can overcome." So reason deserves both our reverence and our suspicion. This inward path has taken us into the whole venture of modern philosophy.

The path also led writers into two modern genres of literature—the novel and biography. Both have explored the limbo between what the writer or the hero thinks and what the world thinks—between "conscience" and "consciousness" (or "joint knowledge"). *Don Quixote,* sometimes called the first modern Western novel, exploits the contrast. And modern biography, unlike Plutarch's *Parallel Lives* of eminent Greeks and Romans, becomes intimate. Of course, while biography and the novel also suffered the temptations of the Public Conscience, they found new ways to dramatize the contrasts between the reality of private vices and the appearance of public virtues, and made literature of the tales of Personal Conscience. A rich vein, pioneered early in this century by Lytton Strachey in his *Eminent Victorians* (1918), has recently been exploited in the United States by Robert Caro's life of Lyndon Johnson, Nigel Hamilton's *JFK,* and many others.

But the Personal Conscience (and consciousness) in the modern West has become more than a resource for the new literary genres of biography and the novel. It has created a vast private realm of literary experience, uncanny new laboratories of the imagination, in what William James in his *Principles of Psychology* (1890) christened "the stream of thought, of consciousness, or of subjective life." In this form "conscience" and "consciousness" converged anew. The most private realm (once called the conscience) would be shared and made public by the writer. In English, the unexcelled modern exponent is, of course, James Joyce (1882–1941). He eloquently announced the convergence in the final words of Stephen Dedalus, "Welcome, O Life! I go to encounter for the millionth time the reality of experience and to forge in the smithy of my soul the uncreated conscience of my race. Old Father, old artificer, stand me now and ever in good stead."

As never before, Montaigne's vision of the self judging the self was realized by Joyce. But there was no escape, even for Joyce, from the myriad perils of the divided self. Each variety of conscientiousness would have its special risks for the writer. We have seen that the Divine Conscience, the conscience of self-proclaimed prophets and authorized ministers to other people's consciences, carried the perils of legalism, pedantry, and casuistry. The Public Conscience carried temptations to polemics, sentimentality, and melodrama. Now the Personal Conscience, refined into the stream of private consciousness, can seduce the writer into a self-sequestered world. Joyce, the conjurer, would demonstrate, like no one before or since, how private, how arcane, how cryptic, the language of Personal Conscience could become. He took us down that road with *The Portrait of the Artist* and *Ulysses,* and then enticed us into the Ultima Thule with *Finnegans Wake.*

To think of the writer as conscience of the world is only to recognize that the writer, as we have seen, is inevitably a divided self, condemned at the same time to express and to communicate, to speak *for* the writer and speak *to* others. To be a writer in the West today, with the experience of these varieties of conscientiousness behind us, challenges us to find new vehicles, new literary forms for the divided self, in a world accustomed to both the Public Conscience and the Personal Conscience.

For the Jew who happens to be living in and writing for a predominantly Christian society, the challenge takes on ever-new interest and new dimensions. Speaking personally, I find that the American experience of being an assimilated grandchild of Orthodox immigrants has tended to make me an ill-informed, nonbelieving, non-observant Orthodox Jew, haunted by nostalgia for the peculiar music of the *shul*, for the Judaism I do not practice. And this adds still another puzzling iridescence to my Jewishness and to the tantalizing opportunities of my writer's divided self.

Looking back through the centuries and the millennia, we can reflect on the unexpectedness of all the past challenges to the writer's divided soul. Each of my three samples of the conscientious experience—the Divine Conscience, the Public Conscience, and the Personal Conscience—was a product of unpredictable forces in history. These included the inspiration of prophets, the appealing claims of a Christian savior, the organized power of a world-reaching church in Rome, the challenge of Protestant reformers—without which the rich literature of the Divine Conscience would be unimaginable. Then the rise of Western industrial society, the technology of printing and the book, and the newspaper and electronic media, along with liberal representative institutions and the progress of literacy and science—all these converged to nourish the powers of public opinion and the reading public—so creating the Public Conscience. And finally, the astonishing creation of the Personal Conscience in this century as a by-product of all the above and countless other unexpected forces—the frustrations of a murderous World War I, the advances of psychology, the invention of psychoanalysis, sexual liberation, and the increasing equality of the sexes.

Each of these stages of the Western conscience has brought unpredicted convergences of conscience and consciousness, with new tests, new trials, and new sources for the ever newly divided self of the writer. May we not be sure that forces at work today will give equally surprising new forms to the writer's divided self in the future?

5

Our Conscience-Wracked Nation

Everybody knows that the founders of New England came here for reasons of conscience. They aimed to "purify" Old World institutions and set up a spiritually pure City upon a Hill. But the European stereotype since the early nineteenth century has depicted the United States as a nation of crass materialists. The word "businessman" in its modern commercial sense, American in origin, came into use around 1830. Alexis de Tocqueville, in the most influential work ever published about the United States, observed that "the love of wealth is . . . to be traced, as either a principal or accessory motive, at the bottom of all the Americans do; this gives to all their passions a sort of family likeness." Travelers, from Charles Dickens to Frances Trollope, documented the portrait of the American philistine. This portrait has, of course, been reinforced by Americans themselves, notoriously in Calvin Coolidge's quip that "the chief business of the American people is business."

This complacent cliché has made it difficult for interested spectators abroad to understand the sources of some of the United States' most troublesome domestic problems in the late twentieth century. These do not come at all from American materialism, questions of cost-effectiveness, or the national deficit. "There is in most Americans," the prescient Justice Louis Brandeis observed in 1953, "some spark of idealism, which can be fanned into a flame. It takes sometimes a divining rod to find what it is; but when found, and that means often, when disclosed to the owners, the results are often extraordinary."

Today we see how those sparks of idealism have been fanned into flame, in a startling renaissance of the New England conscience. In the United States, many of our most widely debated public issues are self-created. We are a people haunted by all past injustices and fears of future injustice. And against these evils we seem driven to find legislative panaceas.

Their robust conscience, the wits tell us, never prevented the early New Englanders from doing whatever they wanted to do. It just kept them from enjoying it. In later centuries the rise of liberal democratic government and majority rule, and the growth of a literate citizenry and a mass-circulation press produced a new arbiter for the conscience—a new voice for God. *Vox populi, vox dei.* And in the United States the Divine Conscience has long since been replaced by the Public Conscience, a force that increasingly haunts and dominates our lives.

Newsmen and politicians in the United States today are overwhelmed by issues of conscience. How can we devise laws, create watchdog commissions, or arouse public outrage to right ancient wrongs that violate our civic conscience? On one sample day (May 19, 1993), the front page of *The Washington Post* featured the following items: a proposed compromise on how to allow homosexuals to serve openly in the military; a young black woman chosen to serve as poet laureate; the first black lawyer with ties to the city nominated for U.S. district attorney; a task-force recommendation that colleges offer more teams and scholarships for women in athletics; and "Health Plan Threatened by Abortion Coverage." The front page of *The New York Times* for the same day featured an opinion poll showing that blacks back Mayor David Dinkins but whites do not, and Hispanics are divided; how the recent voting for school-board members showed people "profoundly roiled" by teaching about sexuality and multiculturalism; an award of $400,000 damages to a City University professor and chairman of the Black Studies Department for his having been demoted for anti-Semitic remarks (expressing satisfaction, the professor called this a victory for "African people"); an illustrated article on the difficulties suffered "When Disabled Students Enter Regular Classrooms."

The Cases of Conscience that exacerbate American political life give no signs of abating in the near future. And these issues of conscience are not imaginary. On the contrary, they are rooted deep in past injustices: blacks enslaved; homosexuals scorned and criminalized; women deprived of opportunities for self-fulfillment; American Indians driven from their lands; handicapped persons denied employment. We Americans today reach out to explore and exploit the frontiers of conscience much as nineteenth-century Americans explored and exploited the physical resources of our vast continent.

Americans have become champions not only of the victims of the gross and conspicuous historic injustices like slavery, but of the victims of countless hidden injustices, like those traditionally suffered by the mentally and physically handicapped. For example, recent laws have not only required ease of access to public buildings and the reconstruction of curbs and sidewalks and access to buses for those confined to wheelchairs, but have mandated employment opportunities. Champions of children's rights have awakened the public to cases of child abuse, and even opened paths to lawsuits by children against their parents. Prosecutions for long-past sexual abuses, real or imagined, are sometimes supported by child witnesses of doubtful reliability. Perhaps the bitterest and most divisive issue in domestic politics—which threatens to give religion a new and menacing role in our civic life—is the issue of abortion. Conscience-stricken citizens cast this issue too in terms of the violation of the "rights" of the unborn. Other Americans, outraged at violations of the purity of the environment, are organized to champion the rights of all animal species to avoid extinction. The survival of the spotted owl and the wolf have thus become substantial polit-

ical issues. And law-review articles have actually been written on
the "rights" of trees.

No one can guess what might be the next Cases of Conscience to
stir Americans' public passions. Many thought that the passage
of the omnibus Civil Rights Act of 1964 banning racial discrimi-
nation in voting, jobs, and public accommodations was the climax of the rights movement. But they underestimated the force
and reach of the New England conscience in the twentieth century. The Civil Rights Act proved to be only one symptom of
what has become an almost pathological hypersensitivity. Recently this protection has been expanded to include penumbral
rights—perilously vague and difficult to define—such as the
rights of women (and men) not to be "sexually harassed." Who
would have predicted that our New World culture of spectacular material successes would offer a melodrama of the sensitive
conscience.

This new American moralism, this renaissance of conscience,
has not been without effect on our culture and our intellectual
and aesthetic standards. Our vocabulary has been revised and
enlarged, presumably to favor every one of the groups that have
become wards of our newly sensitized conscience. The word
"Negro," with a long and respectable history, reinforced in the
titles of scholarly journals and work by champions of racial
equality, became suddenly taboo. For a while "black" was de-
manded, but it was soon displaced by the hyphenated "Afro-
American," or the now-preferred "African-American." Some of
us who have believed the glory of our nation has been our ability
to encompass all comers as Americans are shocked to see any of
our fellow citizens demand to be known as nothing but hyphenated Americans. We should recall Theodore Roosevelt's shrewd
warning in 1915 that "the one absolutely certain way of bringing this nation to ruin, of preventing all possibility of its continuing to be a nation at all, would be to permit it to become a
tangle of squabbling nationalities." While we seem to have es-

caped many Old World ills—religious and linguistic wars, hereditary class distinctions, ideological politics—some citizens seem on the way to making us a Balkan America.

Anyone at his peril would use the outmoded descriptive terms. These are called signs of "bigotry" in a citizen or a newspaper, and are death to a politician. For women, too, one must be scrupulous, as Ms. has become preferred by many as a substitute for Mrs. or Miss. The nomenclature of our First Lady, once a matter of little journalistic concern, has become a minor public issue with the insistent designation of our new First Lady as Hillary Rodham Clinton. "Handicapped" or "otherwise endowed" has become a required euphemism for once-familiar words—blind, deaf, dumb—and the wholly taboo "cripple." The clearly descriptive "homosexual" has been pushed aside by "gay" (first used in this new sense about 1935), which has now lost its wondrous poetic uses, bolstered by the newly coined and polemical "homophobe." In the United States we no longer have the "aged" or "elderly" but only "senior citizens." It may surprise friends abroad to learn that in the United States we have no "ignorant" citizens, but only the "culturally deprived" or "disadvantaged." Nor are there "beggars" here anymore, but only the "homeless." American Indians are no longer Indians but "Native Americans"—to the implicit disparagement of all the rest of us native Americans who were born here. Outrage has been expressed by some citizens of Washington, D.C., at the continued use of "Redskins" as the name of the city's football team. Formerly "exceptional" children were the unusually bright. Now the word gives dignity to those who are exceptional because of their handicaps.

"Ableism" the Smith College Office of Student Affairs in 1990 defined as "oppression of the differently abled, by the temporarily able." And "Lookism" is the sin of "characterizing people by their physical appearance. The belief that appearance is an indicator of a person's value; the construction of a standard for beauty/attractiveness; and oppression through stereotypes and generalizations of both those who do not fit that standard and those who do." But of course we must beware of anything we say in our English language, which one enthusiastic feminist has labeled "Manglish"—"the English language as it is used by men in the perpetuation of male supremacy." To respect female sensitivities, must the once respectable university group called a "seminar" be rechristened an "ovular"? Short people are simply "vertically challenged." Spelling, too, must become more sensitive. I have been roundly reproached for referring to "mankind" or "humanity," and I have been told that "woman" must be respelled "womin" to avoid the offensive inclusion of the male referent.

The effects of our newly sensitized American conscience on our aesthetic and intellectual standards, while hard to measure, have become a sensitive subject in themselves. But surely they have been considerable. The Repatriation Office (established in 1991) of our National Museum of Natural History, one of our principal centers for the study of American Indian ethnography and anthropology, has dismantled its holdings of Native American skeletal remains and funerary or sacred objects, returning some two thousand sets of these to various groups. More than seven hundred sets of such remains were delivered to the native peoples of Larsen Bay, Alaska, where they were packaged and reinterred out of "respect" for their anonymous owners. The birthday of Martin Luther King, Jr., is now our only national holiday to honor a specified person, while the birthdays of Lincoln and Washington have been merged into a single eponymous "Presidents' Day."

What Bertrand Russell once disparaged as "The Superior Virtue of the Underdog" has inevitably diluted our hypersensitive judgments of works of art and literature by all members of the once-victim groups. American schools and universities take it for granted that they can serve their large educational purpose only by relaxing standards to favor the once-disadvantaged.

This practice, not always publicly admitted, is sometimes attacked, but only when it is institutionalized in the form of illegal "affirmative action" and quotas. In recent decades in the United States we have tacitly developed a sliding scale of standards to provide opportunities for those who for whatever reason have in the past been deprived of them. The perils for American culture come less from the application of varied standards than from the pretense that the standards are not being varied, or that there really are no standards anyway. The greatest peril is in the condescension and indignity to disadvantaged groups who are given the message that less should be expected of them, and that they need expect less of themselves.

This age of the hypertrophied conscience has created problems, too, for our traditional politics of majority rule. Instead, we see signs of national institutions similar to the notorious Polish constitution under which any national measure could be vetoed by a single prince. We are in danger of becoming a nation of "minorities" rather than majorities. And the definition of "minority" becomes increasingly vague and elusive. Women, though actually a majority of our population, have acquired the dignity and the claims of a "minority," while, for some reason or other, Jews seem to have lost that claim.

Our fortunately complex constitutional system, which makes it difficult to pass a law, gives ample opportunity for representatives of any of the conscience-benefited groups to prevent legislation they imagine to be to their disadvantage. President Clinton's first nominee for assistant attorney general for civil rights in the Department of Justice has actually suggested the possibility of "granting blacks a minority veto on issues affecting vital minority issues."

Ironically, in the conscientious society, as recent American history shows, the once-victim groups seek not community but "empowerment." And power knows no bounds. They demand compensation for past exclusion, not in the form of full and free admission to the competitive community, but in claims of empowerment to prevent their oppression in the future. The level playing field is not enough.

Yet the level playing field is precisely what America promised to refugees from the Old World. America meant the opportunity to start anew, to build new lives, far from ancestral cemeteries, from family landed estates, from feudal dues, from guild inhibitions. Far, too, from old boundary feuds and linguistic provincialism. But a conscience-wracked nation has no feel for the future. It is unwilling to take the chance that the future may not balance past accounts. It aims to ensure its wards, the disadvantaged, against failure. And can do this only by depriving them of the opportunity to take risks.

Yet ours has been a continent of uncertainties. Hope for the individual has come not only from community but from the willingness to chance competition, to forgo revenge, to give up both claims of ancestral privilege and of compensation for ancestral sufferings. Efforts to cast up the balance sheet of history would have made New World community impossible. American equality could not erase history and would not pretend to, but would only open gates to the future.

III

NEW-WORLD OPPORTUNITIES

Opportunity hath all her hair on her forehead;
when she is past, you may not recall her. She
hath no tuft whereby you can lay hold on her,
for she is bald on the hinder part of her head,
and never returneth again.

—François Rabelais, *Gargantua*

6

Printing and the Constitution

We have been misled by the cliché that ours is the oldest "written" constitution still in use. To be more precise we should call ours probably the first *printed* constitution and surely the oldest printed constitution by which a nation still lives. This puts our constitution in a wider, more modern perspective.

Our nation was born in the bright light of history, and we can trace the framing and detailed revision of this document in the record of the convention that met in Independence Hall in Philadelphia from May 14 to September 17, 1787. Some of the members were men of letters, and all lived in a culture of printed matter. When the Constitutional Convention required a printer, they selected John Dunlap and David C. Claypoole, who had been printers to the Continental Congress since 1776. Their names had appeared on the official printing of the Declaration of Independence in 1776. They had proven their qualifications as the official printers of the Articles of Confederation.

The Framers believed that the strictest secrecy was required to encourage members of the Constitutional Convention to speak their minds freely and to remove temptations to demagoguery. Eleven years earlier, when, once before, the Continental Congress struggled to agree on a new form of government, they had sat in the same room where the Constitutional Convention now met. They then secured the signatures of Dunlap and Claypoole to an oath of secrecy: "We and each of us do swear that we will deliver all the copies of 'the articles of confederation' which we will print together with the copy sheet to the Secretary of Congress and that we will not disclose directly or indirectly the contents of the said confederation." The delegates to the new Constitutional Convention counted on their printers' observing a similar secrecy, and they were not disappointed.

As the work of the convention drew toward a close and the Committee of Detail began putting the convention's decisions into final form, Dunlap and Claypoole regularly supplied members with printed versions of the committee's latest revisions. The first printers' proofs went to the Committee of Detail about August 1 for additional changes. These were incorporated in corrected copy and distributed to all members of the convention probably on August 6. A month later, in early September, the convention as a whole made further revisions, which in turn were incorporated in a new version by the Committee of Detail. This was printed, and referred back to the convention on September 12. "The report was then delivered in at the Secretary's table," recorded the convention's secretary, William Jackson, "and having been once read throughout. Ordered that the Members be furnished with printed copies thereof. The draught of a letter to Congress being at the same time reported—was read once throughout, and afterwards agreed to by paragraphs." On September 14 and 15 the convention went through this revised print section by section. On September 15 Madison noted, "On the question to agree to the Constitution as amended. All the States ay." George Washington wrote in his diary for that day that the convention "adjourned 'till Monday that the Constitution which it was proposed to offer to the People might be engrossed—and a number of printed copies struck off." Dr. James McHenry of Maryland added in his diary that the order was for five hundred copies.

It is plain that in their efforts to give a final form in words to the concepts, arrangements, and compromises on which they had labored for four months the members were always working with *printed* copy. They were continually adding their final changes to these printed versions of their draft constitution. Only at the very end was their joint work finally reduced to "writing," by being "engrossed." The word "engross"—derived from the medieval Latin for large handwriting—in this sense has left our common usage. It is seldom used now except for academic diplomas and certificates of award, wills, deeds, and other legal documents. Then it had a legalistic meaning—"to write out in a peculiar character appropriate to legal documents." By the late eighteenth century this common use of the word had already begun to become obsolete. Printing acquired a new authenticity. The framers of this historic legal document, in fashioning their crucial phrases, were using common printed matter and not a legalistic handwritten text. They were already working with a *printed* constitution.

How otherwise could the convention have done its business— fifty-five delegates conferring, consulting, debating, and agreeing on a specific form of words? For centuries the final form of historic political documents had been "engrossed," to be scrutinized by a few literate and technically competent negotiators. But this document was prepared in close consultation by fifty-five delegates. Could an original text have been reliably transcribed in fifty-five identical copies? Could members have been confident that they were all viewing precisely the same text? Posterity proved that any preposition, comma, colon, or capital letter might hold the fate of the commerce, general welfare, and international relations of a great nation. Without their printed copies they would have been at sea.

The later history of the document was an allegory of the primacy of print. In 1883, when J. Franklin Jameson, eminent American historian and bibliographer and at one time chief of the Manuscript Division of the Library of Congress (1928–37), pursued the "engrossed" copies of our fundamental documents, he found that the engrossed copy of the Declaration of Independence was proudly and conspicuously displayed in the library of the Department of State in Washington. But there at the same time the engrossed handwritten Constitution of the United States "was kept folded up in a little tin box in the lower part of the closet." There was an unintended historic significance in this neglect of the handwritten word. For the gestation and adoption of the Constitution was not in the handwritten but in the printed word. The engrossed Constitution came to the Library of Congress in 1921, where it remained until 1952, when it went to the newly created National Archives. There, displayed in the Great Hall, annually seen by thousands, the handwritten version has finally attained the publicity of print.

There was a significant ambivalence, too, in the very word "engrossed." During the Middle Ages it acquired a second meaning—to buy up the whole stock of something for the purpose of establishing a monopoly. "Engrossing" in both senses is a relic of an old age of monopolies—in knowledge, and in power, too. Printed matter announced a new age, not of "engrossing" but of diffusing.

A historic—and perhaps the first—example of the political implications of printing was the framing, the debating, and the adopting of our Constitution. While it was hardly conceivable that the fifty-five members of the Constitutional Convention could have done their work without the aid of the printing press, it was still less conceivable that without printing the people of thirteen newly independent colonies spread inland from fifteen hundred miles of Atlantic coast could have focused their minds and intelligently debated the document. The Federalist Papers and the other contemporary classics of political debate over the Constitution were themselves by-products—as well as products—of the printing press. Of course, it was a printed version of the Constitution that then provided the common, public focus for their debates.

Unfortunately, Dunlap and Claypoole had to wait five years

to be paid by the new government. Perhaps they were so patient because they had intended to do the job on speculation—hoping to profit from the public curiosity about what the secretive but much-publicized convention had been up to. The Constitutional Convention had been, in James Hutson's apt phrase, "an extraordinary venture in confidentiality." Astonishingly, there were no significant leaks. In our age of "sunshine laws" every private discussion in the councils of government is a potential headline or a feature of nightly newscasters. Resentful bureaucrats prefer to call them "sunburn" laws. When every such council is not an intimate forum but a public sieve, we can wonder whether the incomparable work of the Constitutional Convention could have been accomplished if they had been debating before journalists, newscasters, and a public impatient for controversy and sensation.

The same Framers who scrupulously observed their oaths of secrecy while they were deliberating showed an admirable democratic concern that their product should, in George Washington's phrase, become an "offer to the People"—that it be widely "promulged." The secrecy of their deliberation and the publicity of ensuing discussion were complementary. For centuries historic forces had inevitably confined the arena of interest and debate. Current access to earlier classics of constitutional history—before the spread of literacy—was inevitably limited to the small literate class. The Magna Carta (1215), for example, could not have been debated by more than a tiny fragment of Britons—or even of barons—in its day. Written in Latin, a learned foreign language, the document survived in a few variant handwritten "originals," and entered British constitutional tradition more by rumor and hearsay than by public inspection. The great tradition of an "unwritten" British constitution left the knowledge and the scrutiny of the rights of Britons to judges and lawyers, rather than to the public.

The Constitution of the United States opened a new era in the history of constitutions, not only by its explicit description of the powers of a balanced representative government, but also by its birth in a public forum of the printed word. A widely literate people could read and judge the very words by which they would be governed. The Constitution that emerged from the Philadelphia Convention in mid-September 1787, according to James Madison, "was nothing more than the draft of a plan, nothing but a dead letter, until life and validity were breathed into it by the voice of the people, speaking through the several State Conventions."

"Injunction of secrecy taken off. Members to be provided with printed copies," delegate McHenry noted in his diary on September 17, 1787, "Gentn. of Con. Dined together at the City Tavern." The convention adjourned *sine die* at about four o'clock that afternoon. Secretary Jackson was then to carry copies of the Constitution to the Continental Congress (by now, the Congress of the Confederation) sitting in New York. That night Dunlap and Claypoole were under pressure to make minor revisions ordered at the last session of the convention in time to have the printed copies ready for the New York stage leaving at ten the next morning. Just one hour later the Pennsylvania delegates were scheduled to present the documents to their own legislature. The following afternoon Jackson arrived in New York to deliver the engrossed document and printed copies. On September 20 the Constitution was read to the Continental Congress.

Now at last the public could learn what had been accomplished by their fifty-five delegates who had worked for four months behind closed doors. The printing press would inform the public and bring the Constitution to life. Leonard Rapport's invaluable study of the early printings of the Constitution makes it possible for us to follow the role of the press in making the ensuing public debate possible. Without this diffusion of the printed text, the Constitution might conceivably still have been adopted by the required nine states. But the act never would have had the authority that copious printed publicity would assure. The anti-Federalists had a plausible case for their objection that the convention had exceeded its authority. Anti-Federalist sentiments were widespread. If copies of the Constitution had not been broadly diffused (how else if not in print?), they would have given substance to suspicions that the Federalists were trying to overwhelm opposition by speed and surprise. In the result, however, full and accurate printed copies of the Constitution broadcast by newspapers in every state made it hard to argue that anyone had been deprived of the opportunity to object. Of course, the suffrage at the time was much narrower than it is today. But in due course, literacy and other printed matter would play a role in changing that, too.

The general diffusion of printed texts of the new Constitution thus helped set a tone of fairness and decency—and declared the freedom to object—at the very adoption of our frame of government. Is it any wonder that Jefferson, who would take his lumps from the press, ventured that "The basis of our government being the opinion of the people, the very first object should be to keep that right; and were it left to me to decide whether we should have a government without newspapers, or newspapers without government, I should not hesitate a moment to prefer the latter." Unfortunately, Americans in the later twentieth century would see tragic allegories of Jefferson's point in great nations with powerful governments but no free newspaper press. They would see that, but for the freedom to print, there could be no "consent of the governed."

In September and October 1787 Americans learned about their proposed Constitution mainly through the newspaper press. The copies sent to the states for formal submission to their ratifying conventions, Leonard Rapport has shown, were actually produced as a newspaper supplement. In New York the twice-a-week *Independent Journal,* published by John McLean, enthusiast for the new Constitution, regularly devoted three of its four pages to advertisements and only the remaining page to news. To print the full text of the Constitution he would have had to cut the advertisements. Therefore he printed the whole Constitution as a separate four-page *Supplement to the Independent Journal,* dated Saturday, September 22. To correct errors and omissions in his text he put the *Supplement* through three revisions and finally in a fourth revision added the resolutions of Congress of September 28 and the letter transmitting the report of the convention to the states. Copies of this fourth version of the *Supplement,* attested by Charles Thomson, secretary of the Continental Congress, survive in the official archives of New York and North Carolina. It was on this printed version that the state ratifying conventions deliberated and cast their votes. There is good reason to dignify this *Supplement* to a semiweekly newspaper as "the printed archetype of the Constitution."

In the new age of typography it was not the uniqueness of an "engrossed" copy sequestered in some archive but the publicity of print that gave authenticity and authority to acts of government. Newspaper publishers were earnest, energetic, and ingenious in their efforts to sate readers' appetites for the authentic product of the secretive convention. On September 26, Benjamin Russell, publisher of *The Massachusetts Centinel,* offered the full text of the Constitution and boasted to his readers: "The following HIGHLY INTERESTING and IMPORTANT communication was received late last evening by the post—an ardent desire to gratify the patrons of the Centinel, and the publick in general, induced the Editor to strain a nerve that it might appear this day; and although lengthy he is happy in publishing the whole entire, for their entertainment." Nor did publishers allow profit to stand in their way. On September 28, the weekly Winchester *Virginia Gazette,* whose advertising revenues normally came to between six and eight dollars an issue, sacrificed all but one seventy-five-cent advertisement to make space for the full text of the Constitution. The *New York Journal* (September 27) apologized to readers for omitting "a number of advertisements, pieces and paragraphs . . . to give place to the Federal Constitution," and so, too, did the Providence *United States Chronicle.*

It took some time for the printed word to get around. While newspaper versions speedily multiplied in the Northeast and New England, it was Tuesday, October 2, before the printed text appeared south of Virginia. This was in an *Extraordinary,* a supplement to the semiweekly Charleston *Columbian Herald,* to which a ship had brought a copy of the text by an eleven-day passage from Philadelphia. On the remote frontier, in "the town of Lexington in the District of Kentucke," John Bradford's weekly *Kentucke Gazette* offered the full text of the Constitution in three installments beginning October 20.

Newspaper publishers tried various expedients. The *Norwich Packet* in Connecticut offered the text in two installments. The publisher of the *New-York Morning Post* and *Hutchins Improved Almanack* for 1788 advertised in the *Post* that a full four-page text of the Constitution was being inserted in his almanac, because it was "highly expedient" that everyone should have a copy of the proposed new Constitution, and "those who wish to possess themselves with one, have now an opportunity with the advantage of an Almanack into the Bargain." Others printed the Constitution in handbills and pamphlets.

Considering the length of the Constitution—more than five thousand words—the cost of hand-setting, the scarcity of paper, and the small size of newspapers at the time, to provide readers so promptly with the full text of so technical a document would demonstrate an impressive public spirit. Of about eighty newspapers publishing in the colonies at the time, by October 6—only twenty days after the convention had adjourned—at least fifty-five had printed the full text. By the end of October the participating newspapers numbered some seventy-five. Even before Delaware, the first state, met in its ratifying convention on December 3, the number of separate printings of the Constitution in newspapers or other formats came (according to Rapport's count) to more than one hundred and fifty.

We can never know precisely how many printings were made of the full text of the Constitution before it was ratified. The multiplication of copies by print made knowledge more than ever uncontrollable, unaccountable, incalculable. The dissemination of print dramatized the mysterious powers of knowledge and its uncanny capacity to increase by diffusion. In a free American society the printing press made it possible for citizens to have access to the most significant public facts in privacy and at their convenience. Unlike a unique engrossed document, to which access could be controlled, printed copies spread with the wind. No one could know for sure who had read what, or when, or what any reader had found in it for himself. The multiplying copies of the *printed* proposed Constitution were symbols of an opening society in which eventually all would have a right to know and judge the public business.

The appearance in our dictionaries of the Soviet word *samizdat* in the mid-twentieth century to describe "dangerous" printed matter clandestinely circulated is an ominous reminder that governments can retreat from the modern age of free public print to the dark age when public documents were "engrossed" for only a privileged few. Thomas Carlyle's familiar observation that the art of printing "was disbanding hired armies, and cashiering most kings and senates, and creating a whole new democratic order" is no longer a platitude. The story of the adoption of our Constitution can now more than ever remind us that our frame of government was born in the freedom to print and to read.

The printed publicity of the debate over the Constitution carried still another historic message. As Dunlap and Claypoole and McLean printed and corrected their successive versions of the text, they were reminded that its words were the work of fallible men. The odor of sanctity, the aura of divinity, the historic inevitability that despots have always claimed for their self-serving laws, were being dissolved. Men were here reminded of their responsibility for their laws, their powers to make and shape their own constitution. What men had made, they could improve. The explicit provision for amendment, a characteristically American feature, proved essential to the longevity of our Constitution. Printing the Constitution reminded men that their laws were not the creation of a uniquely sacred "engrossing" legal hand, but the product of public information and agreement on what everybody could know.

Public print, especially newspaper print, was the clearest testimony that the institutions of government were only human, always improvable, and so always perfectible. Sharing this hope, we hear Benjamin Franklin's wise advice at the close of the Constitutional Convention: "Thus I consent, Sir, to this Constitution, because I expect no better, and because I am not sure it is not the best. The opinions I have had of its errors I sacrifice to the public good. . . . I hope, therefore, for our own sakes, as a part of the people, and for the sake of our posterity, that we shall act heartily and unanimously in recommending this Constitution, wherever our influence may extend, and turn our future thoughts and endeavors to the means of having it well administered."

7

Roles of the President's House

Democracies—and especially ours in the United States—despite many strengths, are conspicuously weak in ritual. Yet ritual, a public ceremonial affirmation of community, satisfies a need felt in all societies. In our country the only ritual required by our Constitution is the president's inauguration. This suggests the special aura, a democratic aura, that surrounds our president. And as it surrounds his inauguration, his ceremonial entering on his duties as the only public servant selected by the whole citizenry, so too it surrounds his residence.

Time alone is the resource that can enrich ritual and give it meaning. Yet this is the one resource in which we in the United States are not especially rich. But in our democratic New World society architecture can and does play the role of ritual. It can do this because architecture has many of the features of ritual:

1. It is structured.

2. It can be dramatic.

3. It provides a repetitive experience that ties us to the past.

4. It is communal, emphasizing and embodying the relation of people to one another and to their common past.

5. It is capable of embellishment, renewal, and subtle change.

6. It is durable and can outlive the generations.

Architecture, too, has the advantage over ritual in not requiring a priesthood or even a leading human performer to make its impact. Its separation from any individual affirms the prime importance of the community and the product over the interests of any one leader or generation. Also, by contrast with ritual it suggests and affirms the *material* foundations of community.

In some conspicuous ways our distinctive history has given an especially revealing role to our architecture. American mobility, for example, was vividly embodied in our first characteristic domestic architecture. This was not the log cabin, which was a New World version of an older Swedish design. It was the balloon-frame house. An American contrivance, quickly built and quickly demounted for removal to some distant place, the balloon frame of planks nailed together was invented in our West for impatient and ambitious Americans who might want to move from Chicago to Omaha and beyond. It first appeared prominently in Chicago in 1833 and would continue to serve American needs for speedy construction by people who lacked the Old World mortise-and-tenon skills of cabinetmaker, joiner, or carpenter. It was destined to become the pioneering design for American suburbia.

In these Western communities of transients and boosters, architecture also provided prominent symbols of community pride, rivalry, hospitality, and expansiveness. The hotel was one of the most distinctive and remarkable of these American architectural symbols, marking the birth and optimistic spirit of newly founded cities across the continent. The hotel was complemented by other speedily built monuments to the pride of new communities—county courthouses and grandiose state capitols. Then, in the later nineteenth century, catastrophe (such as the Chicago Fire of 1871) and commercial opportunity led American businessmen to create peculiarly American "cathedrals of commerce," better known as skyscrapers. These became symbols of the boundless heavenward aspiration of a technologically inspired democratic nation.

But architecture also has had a political significance and symbolism, which was brilliantly illustrated in Great Britain during

World War II in the too-little-celebrated observations of the prophetic Winston Churchill. After a German bomb struck the
House of Commons on May 10, 1941, the House debated the
question of how to rebuild. The House was oblong in shape, and
some suggested that it be rebuilt in a semicircular form. To this
Churchill strenuously objected. He stood firm for the original
oblong in which it had been constructed after the fire of 1834.

As usual Churchill's reasons were interesting and based on
broad principles. He explained that it was because he favored
the party system of government (as against what he called the
"group" system). In a semicircular chamber, he explained, "it is
easy for an individual to move through those insensible grada-
tions from left to right, but the act of crossing the floor [of a
rectangular chamber] is one which requires serious consideration."

Churchill also urged that the new building not be too large,
for, he said, "a small chamber and a sense of intimacy are indis-
pensible." Surprisingly, Churchill even insisted that the recon-
structed House of Commons building "should not be big
enough to contain all its members at once without overcrowd-
ing, and that there should be no question of every Member having a separate seat reserved for him." Otherwise, he said,
nine-tenths of the time the Debates will be "in the depressing
atmosphere of an almost empty or half-empty chamber." Such a
design was necessary to preserve the traditional atmosphere of
the House, which "has lifted our affairs above the mechanical
sphere into the human sphere." This is an observation that we
too may fairly make of our White House.

In any event, Churchill urged, it was crucial that the House of
Commons be rebuilt as soon as possible—on old foundations
and in the old dimensions. There must be no danger of the
House not having its place of meeting. "I rank the House of
Commons," he declared, "—the most powerful Assembly in the
whole world—at least as important as a fortification or a battle-
ship even in time of war." Churchill's irresistible eloquence per-

suaded his colleagues that only such a building would give the public business of the Parliament "a sense of Crowd and Urgency." The ever-fluent Churchill ended his speech by thanking the House of Lords for letting the Commons meet in its "spacious, splendid hall . . . under this gilded, ornamented, statue-bedecked roof." And it is interesting for our present purposes that he concluded:

> Mid pleasures and palaces though we may
>   roam,
> Be it ever so humble, there's no place like
>   home.

We surely would not want the residence of our president to convey what Churchill wanted for the House of Commons—"a sense of Crowd and Urgency." We would prefer a sense of intimacy and informality. But we can say much more than that. For our White House, our president's house, like the House of Commons, has carried and can continue to carry some special meanings for our society and our government.

I was recently and vividly reminded of these special meanings when I visited another history-laden set of buildings that also long served as the residence of a head of state. It too takes its name from its color. And by its stark contrasts it may help us understand the meanings of our White House.

The building that I found so redolent of contrasts is the famous Red House, or Alhambra. It is so called from the Arabic word for red, the color of the sun-dried bricks, made of fine gravel and clay, of its outer walls. Built on a hill on the outskirts of Granada in southern Spain, it served as official residence of the Nasrid kings of Granada for some two hundred and fifty years—from about 1240 to 1492—a half century longer than our White House has yet served as the residence of our presidents. And with its 2,000 servants and court officials its staff somewhat exceeded the 1,575 employees (at latest count) in the Executive Office of the President (including 88 in the executive residence). Like our White House, the Alhambra was a combination office and residence. Although the physical expanse of the Alhambra impresses us with its vast extent, the White House grounds are hardly meager, covering some eighteen acres.

Some might be outraged by this comparison of the works of an absolute Moorish potentate with those of our popularly elected, constitutionally limited president. But the outlandish contrast of the roles of these two architectural metaphors can help us discover the distinctive roles of our White House. As I visited the exotic Alhambra's storied halls and walls and towers and gardens and enjoyed its exotic charms, it seemed to provide me with a vivid and suggestive metaphor for what our White House is not. By contrast, the Alhambra brought into high relief three grand and simple features of our president's house, as clues to our whole scheme of government.

Of these the most obvious and perhaps most American is *accessibility*. The Alhambra, like other residences of rulers, is a palace in a castle. Old World rulers, needing protection from foreign invaders, rival princes, and discontented subjects, naturally ensconced themselves and their court behind high walls and moats, securely defended by heavily fortified towers. A familiar example is Windsor Castle, a fortified royal residence from Saxon times (c. ninth century). The need for this protection is attested by the beautifully preserved filigreed royal palace in the Alhambra buttressed by the massive walls and towers of the Alcazaba, the adjoining military quarters, several times destroyed and rebuilt. It is not surprising that uneasy absolute rulers should dwell in a fortress-palace.

Nor is it surprising that our elected president, living in a house that the citizens consider to be their gift and their property, should be at ease with his people and give them ready access to his home. Where else can a citizen go to his elected representative and secure a ticket allowing him to enter and tour the actual present residence of the head of state and government? Whenever I drive past the White House and see the lines of Americans of all ages and no special status waiting for their tour of the house they have provided for their elected chief public servant, I am reminded of how distinctive are our American institutions. Regal residences in other times and places have been closely guarded against the vulgar eyes and muddy feet of the populace.

But our White House is an emphatically public residence, which some of its tenants have discovered to their irritation. Presidents have reacted differently to the pains of living in a public facility. "It seems like there was always somebody for supper," President Truman complained. But while President Reagan observed, "You get a little stir-crazy during the week," he good-naturedly added that living in the White House reminded him of his early experience—"Now, here I am," he said, "sort of living above the store again." But some who never had the opportunity to live there solaced themselves with its trials. General William T. Sherman did in his often quoted quip, "If forced to choose between the penitentiary and the White House for four years, I would say the penitentiary, thank you."

Another too easily forgotten feature embodied in our White House is *civility*. Just as the deliberations of both houses of our Congress have been remarkably decorous—with none of the throwing of ink bottles and screaming of epithets found in parliamentary bodies of some other countries—so, except for rare lapses, our presidents have generally treated their opponents and have been treated by their opponents with restraint and decorum.

The Anglo-American poet W. H. Auden once observed that the most remarkable feature of an American presidential election is that on election night none of the candidates—win or lose—would be packing his baggage to leave the country. This is not a universal feature of presidential elections around the world. But civility has remained a robust American political tradition embodied in the conduct of presidential life in the White House.

I was reminded of this by a melodramatic episode of the Alhambra that for me provided an edifying if exotic tale of contrasts, which no visitor to the Alhambra is apt to forget. This tale attaches to one of the more picturesque rooms, the so-called Abencerrajes Gallery, leading on to the famous Court of the Lions of unsurpassed elegance. Here, according to legend, the ruthless King Boabdil sometime in the 1480s summoned the thirty-six leaders of the rival Abencerrajes family for a peace-making banquet. But he seized the occasion to dispose of them by beheading all thirty-six. He then tossed their heads into the central basin beneath the Moorish ceiling with its fantastic stalactites and its charming star-shaped lantern cupola. The red stains still visible in the central basin are said by some to come from the iron oxide in the marble, and said by others to be the indelible bloody marks of the decapitated heads. Some historians attribute this massacre not to Boabdil but to his father, yet there remains substance to the story.

Despite the sometimes bitter rivalries of American party politics, the halls of the White House have remained quite unbloody. Burned by the British in 1814, it was rebuilt and extended in the next decade. Although we have suffered several assassinations of our presidents, none of these has occurred in or even near the White House. The only notorious occasion of conspicuous disorder in the president's residence has been the familiar inaugural reception for President Andrew Jackson in March 1829. Then, as William Seale vividly recounts, Democracy came to the White House with a vengeance. The crowds surging into the oval drawing room pushed President Jackson against the wall until he gasped for breath. Some friends had the presence of mind to help him escape through a window onto the south portico and then to the ground, and took him off to refuge where he had been staying, in Gadsby's hotel. The *Washington City Chronicle* blandly reported that "the President's hospitality on this occasion was in some measure misapplied." There was no loss of life, but considerable loss of "the dignity of the Presidency as well as the character of the nation." "But it was the People's day," one witness recorded, "and the People's President and the People would rule. . . . The noisy and disorderly rabble in the President's House brought to my mind descriptions I had read, of the mobs in the Tuileries and at Versailles." But there were no beheadings, no guillotine, and even this sort of mild disorder by thirsty Washingtonians would not be repeated. It became only another example of the distinctive openness of the president's residence in a democracy.

This unusual episode suggests still another continuing feature of the architectural symbolism of the White House. I have mentioned *accessibility* and *civility,* and a third is *representativeness.* Compared with the official residences of the famous heads of other great nations, the White House is a prosaic place. With his *Tales of the Alhambra* (1832) Washington Irving (1783–1859), sometimes called the first American author to acquire an international reputation, provided us with a minor American classic embroidering the history and legends of that famous Red House of kings. The chapters of that book, mostly written while he stayed in a room in the royal palace of the Alhambra, still strike us with their poetic redolence of the buildings, the architecture, the decoration, and their history. As Irving watched "the declining daylight upon this Moorish pile, I was led into a consideration of the light, elegant and voluptuous character prevalent throughout its internal architecture and to contrast it with the grand but gloomy solemnity of the Gothic edifices, reared by the Spanish conquerors. The very architecture thus bespeaks the opposite and irreconcilable natures of the two warlike peoples who so long battled for the mastery of the Peninsula." And Irving was similarly inspired when he viewed the Alhambra by moonlight. "I have sat by hours at my window, inhaling the sweetness of the garden and musing on the chequered fortunes of those whose history is dimly shadowed out in the elegant memorials around." Although the White House has now stood for two centuries in a literate city of countless authors in a world whose fortunes have been shaped by the inhabitants of the president's house, we have yet to see any counterpart to Irving's work. We know no *Tales of the White House*. Nor are we apt to.

The reason is a prime feature of this distinctly American architectural metaphor, what I call its *representativeness*. As our political system has been designed not to give power to men of charisma but to allow the nation to be governed by representative men, our White House offers the nation a scene of a president and his family leading lives not dissimilar to our own. It is a prosaic prospect, but one that elevates us citizens by reminding us that our president leads a life essentially similar to ours, in surroundings not resplendent and sumptuous but grand and comfortable. Some of the more discriminating tenants of the White House have noted how much the president's house resembles everybody else's house. Jacqueline Kennedy, reflecting on the prospect of her family's move into the White House, observed, "It looks like it's been furnished by discount stores." After she moved in, a perceptive reporter observed that "she changed the White House from a plastic to a crystal bowl."

The dignity and decorum of daily life in the president's house can be contagious. The features that conspicuously reach the citizenry remind us less of the grandeur than of the commonplaceness of the resident president's life—the affection for children and grandchildren, and dogs, the Thanksgiving dinner, the Christmas tree, the family birthday parties. Not even Walt Whitman could be inspired by its commonplaceness, and the White House remains our most prosaic national monument.

In expressing the openness of American public life—with a convenient office for the press, in a society with sunshine laws that allow all citizens the right to scrutinize government records—the White House, too, symbolizes a democratic refusal to distinguish between the public and the private. During the president's incumbency we expect him to make the White House his *home,* his place of family living. A continual public view of the president's life in the White House is provided by the president's photographer. The work of the remarkable Yoichi Okamoto, for example, has provided the public with an unprecedented copious and comprehensive view of the life of a president. The men and women of the press, too, have become integral members of the White House family, symbolized by the newly convenient facilities provided them in the White House Press Room, which one reporter recently described as "an adult day-care center."

Because our president is both head of state and head of government, special symbolic demands were made on the planners. The siting of the house itself succeeded in expressing the more obvious distinctive features of our constitutional government. This, again, is in contrast to the situation in Great Britain or France, where the head of state is a separate and ceremonial person. When President Washington and Major L'Enfant chose two commanding sites a mile and a half apart for the House of Congress in the Capitol and for the president's house, they dramatized the separation of legislative and executive powers found in the Constitution. In Philadelphia, where the federal government had been before the move to Washington, this dramatic symbolism had been lacking. There the Congress had been meeting next door to Independence Hall, only a few blocks from the president's house. And after the president delivered his address to the Congress, the members walked or rode in rented coaches to the nearby house where the president was lodged. The occasion was not properly expressive either of the separation of powers or of the dignity of the occasion.

The move to Washington gave Pierre Charles L'Enfant (1754–1825) his chance to plan a proper capital for the new nation for whose creation he had fought and been wounded as a volunteer engineer serving at his own expense. L'Enfant seized his assignment with imagination, energy, and every virtue except discretion. He refused to accept advice, and when he saw a house obstructing a street that he had planned, without any legal authority he simply tore it down. Unfortunately it belonged to an influential citizen, and this among other indiscretions caused the termination of his services on February 27, 1792.

L'Enfant, born in Paris, had a vision of capitals influenced by his view of Versailles. The frustration of his hopes, too, would reveal the distinctive role of the president's house in a New World constitutional democracy. As William Seale has observed, L'Enfant had fixed on locating legislative and executive branches on two widely separated eminences. And he probably designed Pennsylvania Avenue (having in mind the ceremonial processions of European monarchs along boulevards lined by their cheering subjects) as a long grand avenue to give still more dignity and emphasis to the separation of president from Congress. L'Enfant must have imagined a procession of state coaches drawn by richly caparisoned horses, carrying an impressive array of dignitaries. But when the avenue had its first trial, after President Adams addressed a joint session of the Congress on November 22, 1800, the effect was not impressive. Members of Congress made their way laboriously to the new president's house through a sea of mud, in miscellaneous vehicles, mostly hacks hired off the streets. Later Congress passed a law to pave a walkway from the Capitol to the president's house. But L'Enfant's imagined grand procession after the president's address to the joint meetings of Congress never took place. Still, L'Enfant's vision was not entirely unfulfilled, for his Grand Avenue—Pennsylvania Avenue—did become the memorable scene for dramatizing the one American political ritual, the inauguration of the president. Later generations would preserve their distinctive images of each inauguration by the spectacle on that avenue of incoming and outgoing presidents.

What is the future role of the White House in American life and culture? In my view, its role nowadays as a historic place and monument of our traditions is more significant than ever.

And it becomes more necessary with every advance in our technology. For the new media of the last century have tended to dissolve our sense of place and of time. "Is it live or is it taped?" When and where? Fewer and fewer places and times preserve their uniqueness, as we are overwhelmed by photography, movies, television, videotapes, television documentaries, and recorded messages.

Then the question for us today is: Can the White House remain a place that reassures us by making vivid the ties of our democratic government to individual living people with all their weaknesses, their warmth, and informality?

8

The Making of a Capitol

We are fortunate to possess an elegant architectural metaphor for our political visions and hopes—our national Capitol. The British, with whom we share the traditions of representative government, have not been nearly so fortunate. For most of the last century the Houses of Parliament have met in a building of the Gothic Revival, a picturesque but irrelevant reach for a long-past era, rebuilt after it was struck by German bombs in World War II. But our Capitol survives from its beginning as a brilliant symbol both of the aspirations of our nation's founders and of the capacity of representative government to adapt to an expanding nation and an advancing technology.

The Capitol, as the traditional stage for the only ritual required by our Constitution—the president's inauguration—has become a witness and a symbol of continuity. So, too, our Capitol gives order and dignity to our political memories as a traditional dramatic setting for our repeating communal experience, the sessions of our Congress. And our national Capitol has dramatized the paradox of a New World nation living by the most venerable written constitution still in use, in a building that faithfully embodies the tastes and hopes of its founders.

The government of this new nation would be centered in the first city expressly built to be a nation's capital. The city planner chosen by George Washington, the French-born Pierre Charles

L'Enfant, as we have seen, had in mind a kind of new Paris of boulevards, vistas, and parks, and with the added charms of Versailles. Ironically his plan became a capital city quite unlike any of its Old World counterparts. One of his unexpected achievements was also to provide the setting for a national Capitol without precedent.

The Constitution in 1787 (Article I, Section 8) had given Congress power over a capital District "(not exceeding ten miles square) as may, by cession of particular States, and the acceptance of Congress, become the seat of the government of the United States." There is no persuasive evidence that George Washington himself shaped this provision. But his choice of the Potomac region undoubtedly was affected by his familiarity with the countryside of his family residence on the Potomac. For Congress, the association of the area with George Washington was important, perhaps decisive.

The choice of the site on the Potomac can remind us of how dramatically the dimensions of national aspirations have changed in the last two centuries. In that age of slow and cumbersome overland travel, it was assumed that the seat of government for this nation of Atlantic colonies should be an Atlantic port city. And of possible sites, a location on the Potomac River seemed at the time to offer ready access to the Ohio Valley and the adjacent West, where the nation was expected to expand. This hope became a practical reality in 1784 with the organization of the Potomac Company, dedicated to boosting inland navigation, with charters and a grant of £6,666 each from Virginia and Maryland. George Washington was its first president. The company aimed to raise private funds to build canals connecting the Potomac with the Ohio River. So the Potomac would be a headquarters for the young nation's expansive westward hopes. Textbook accounts, looking backward from the Civil War, emphasize the choice of the site as a sectional compromise between North and South and an omen of the conflict to come. But we must not forget that in the minds of those who made the decision and passed the Residence Act in 1790, the future of a westward-expanding nation loomed large. And the hopes of George Washington himself commanded respect.

When the three commissioners selected by George Washington chose L'Enfant to plan the new city and fix the locations of the principal buildings, the obvious place for the Capitol was a high point then known as Jenkins' Hill. L'Enfant called it "a pedestal waiting for a monument." After the arrogant L'Enfant was dismissed in 1792, the commissioners announced a competition for the design of a building for this site. The prize was five hundred dollars and a city lot.

It proved much easier to fix the Capitol's site than to settle on its design. The difficulties reveal the problems and opportunities of a new transatlantic nation separated from the sources of European culture. President Washington wrote to Secretary of State Thomas Jefferson that the Capitol "ought to be upon a scale far superior to any thing in *this* Country." Only a domed building, Washington insisted, would have the required grandeur and elegance. Since there were no domed structures in the country at the time, Washington could only have seen them in illustrations. Still the Dome had already become a popular American metaphor for the Constitution—a "beauteous Dome" providing "a great Federal Superstructure," supported by the thirteen states and in turn protecting them. An enthusiastic poet, Benjamin Russell, in his "Birth of Columbia" in 1788, had already imagined:

> Behold the FEDERAL DOME majestick
>   rise!
> On lofty Pillars rear'd, whose ample base,
> On firm foundations laid, unmov'd shall
>   stand,
> 'Till happy your unnumbered circles run,
> The TEMPLE OF CELESTIAL LIBERTY!

While warning against "extravagance" in public buildings, the prudent Washington wanted "a chaste plan sufficiently capacious and convenient for a period not *too* remote, but one to which we may *reasonably* look forward." Some sixteen entries in the architectural competition for the Capitol have survived, but none could satisfy these hopes.

The versatile Thomas Jefferson took an active interest. He had been designing his own home at Monticello, and had recently designed the capitol of Virginia on the model of a classic temple. Jefferson now urged a similar design on one of the competitors, Stephen Hallet, a French architect living in Philadelphia. But Hallet could not adapt Jefferson's Virginia design to the larger scale of a national Capitol. Jefferson then suggested a spherical model, of which the Pantheon in Rome seemed the most perfect example and the Panthéon in Paris seemed the most suitable to the American site. Jefferson himself made some sketches, but Hallet could not translate them into a suitable plan for the building. Still, the basic scheme—a central dome with wings—would become the style of American state capitols.

The outcome of the competition for the design of the Capitol was symbolic. The winner was no architect of distinction but an amateur—the thirty-three-year-old William Thornton (1759–1828), born in a community of the Society of Friends in one of the Virgin Islands. He had been trained as a physician in Scottish universities, but had never practiced medicine. He had become an American citizen in 1788, had lived in Philadelphia, and had designed a new building for the Library Company there. Thornton recalled how, with the rashness of the amateur, he had made his first-prize-winning design. "When I travelled, I never thought of architecture. But I got some books and worked a few days, then gave a plan in the ancient Ionic order, which carried the day." He had already proven his inventive imagination when in 1778 he had begun collaborating with John Fitch on his pioneer design for steamboats operated by paddles. Fitch's third boat, named the *Thornton*, reaching a speed of eight miles an hour, had made the regular packet run on the Delaware River until it was retired in 1790. After Fitch's widely publicized success, Thornton published his own *Short Account of the Origin of Steam Boats* (1814), supporting Fitch's (and his own) claims to credit.

Thornton's versatility was astonishing. His skills as a draftsman and artist helped persuade people to adopt his architectural plans. He won a medal from the American Philosophical Society for his treatise on the elements of written language, and he left three unpublished novels. He wrote a pioneer work on teaching the deaf and was active in antislavery movements. He also tried to found a national university in Washington. Among his grander visions was a union of the two American continents, with a capital near Panama and a canal uniting the two oceans.

The first grandiose project to incite Thornton's imagination was the design for the new United States Capitol. When he heard of the competition he was back in Tortola, and from there he wrote the commissioners offering to bring them his plan. Arriving in Washington, after a glimpse of Hallet's efforts to embody Jefferson's themes, he produced a new version. When President Washington voiced enthusiasm for the "grandeur, simplicity and convenience" of Thornton's still-unfinished plan, this ensured its adoption. Jefferson too praised Thornton's plan as "simple, noble, beautiful, excellently distributed, and moderate in size." While Thornton was awarded the five hundred dollars and the city lot, Hallet received an equal sum as consolation.

But since Thornton was neither a professional architect nor a builder, Hallet was engaged to supervise the construction. President Washington regretted that neither the practicality nor the cost of Thornton's plan had been studied before it was adopted. So, to ensure speedy construction, the president charged Secretary of State Jefferson with modifying the plan to make it feasible and less costly. Under Jefferson's direction Thornton's plan was "reformed" and "reduced into practicable form" approved by Washington and the commissioners, and work on the foundation began. On September 18, 1793, the cornerstone was laid by Washington himself. Jefferson, whose architectural ideas would be embodied in the building, but who had no taste for ceremony, was not present.

"Thornton's plan," an emphatically collaborative product, provided the basic features that survived the two following centuries. This was a central dome facing east and west, flanked by two balanced wings extending north and south. This simple essential concept remarkably weathered the changing views of several architects, lack of funds, perils of fire, wartime shortages and destruction, and it proved capable of expansion to meet the needs of a vastly larger nation.

The architects engaged on the Capitol during these two centuries are a rough epitome of American architectural history before the skyscraper. Only the Gothic Revival is not represented. Jefferson engaged the architect-engineer Benjamin H. Latrobe (1764–1820), a leader of the Greek Revival who had assisted him with detail on the capitol in Richmond, to build the South Wing and to rebuild after the whole structure had been left "a most magnificent ruin" from fires set by British troops on August 24, 1814. Among his innovations was a column with a tobacco-leaf capital. After Latrobe's departure in 1817, President Monroe hired Charles Bulfinch (1763–1844). Often called the first American professional architect, Bulfinch was already noted for his design of the Massachusetts State House in Boston, and his designs dominated New England public buildings. During his years as Architect of the Capitol (1817–30) Bulfinch designed the Rotunda, improved and redesigned many details, and finished the construction with the East Portico in 1826.

By 1850 the expansion of the nation and the need for more space in the Capitol led to a competition in the charge of the Senate Committee on Public Buildings (Senator Jefferson Davis of Mississippi, chairman) for designs to extend the building. Again the prize was five hundred dollars (but no city lot). When no clear winner was found, the money was split several ways. To design the extension (for which Congress had made an initial appropriation of one hundred thousand dollars), President Millard Fillmore appointed a fellow Whig, Thomas U. Walter (1811–1876), of Philadelphia. Walter, son of a bricklayer and himself a master bricklayer, had engineering experience and had trained under William Strickland (1788–1854), a master of the Greek Revival style. During his years as Architect of the Capitol (1851–65), Walter expanded and rebuilt much of the structure to its present form. Drawing on the suggestions of others, his extension of the Capitol took the form of two large wings at right angles to the existing building and connected to the north and south ends of the existing building by narrow corridors. These extensions too were thoroughly in the classical tradition of the original structure. The ritual symbolism of the Capitol was flamboyantly declaimed by Daniel Webster in a two-hour-long oration at the laying of the cornerstone of the extensions on July 4, 1851. The new wings joined to the old stood for the new states (Texas, California, New Mexico) and the promise of still more to come—proclaiming that the Union, like the Capitol, "may endure for ever!" Ironically it was Jefferson Davis, President Franklin Pierce's able secretary of war and later president of the Confederacy, who as senator had helped secure the first appropriations for the extensions and now directed the work. Through Montgomery C. Meigs, a strong-minded captain in the Corps of Engineers, Davis took an intimate interest in the new construction, commissioning works of art and trying to increase the elegance of the interior.

A spark from a stove on Christmas Eve, 1851, which set off a fire that gutted the Library of Congress in the west-central building, would, surprisingly, put this grand Greek Revival Capitol in the vanguard of American technology. When Walter rebuilt the Library in the Capitol he constructed the first room in America of fireproof cast iron. There the Library remained until its removal across the street to its elegant neo-Renaissance building in

1897. The Library fire would decisively affect the grand silhouette and future shape of the Capitol, for it aroused fears that a fire igniting Bulfinch's wooden dome might engulf the whole building. Walter seized the opportunity to replace, elevate, and modernize Bulfinch's dome. The extensions of the Capitol had dwarfed Bulfinch's dome, and besides offering a fire hazard, the old dome leaked.

For his new dome the practical-minded Walter, trained in the neoclassical tradition, found impressive models in Europe—St. Peter's Basilica in Rome, St. Paul's Cathedral in London, the Panthéon in Paris, and St. Isaac's Cathedral in St. Petersburg. For his radical innovation—a double dome—there was European precedent in the Panthéon in Paris. Assisted by modern American industrial technology, the bold Walter saw that a double dome could solve several problems at once. His concept was an inner dome of stone within a frame of cast iron that would be covered on the outside by stone masonry in the neoclassical style. So he imagined a high dome of unprecedented grandeur and elegance. Incidentally, in the Rotunda this would provide space for a monumental painting on some grand American theme to cover the eye of the inner dome.

It was cast iron, surprisingly, that would finally make this inspiring stone monument possible. The old foundation of Bulfinch's Rotunda could not have supported the weight of a high dome of solid stone. But the newly developed cast iron provided a much lighter frame for a dome soaring above the old one. Some in Congress and the architectural profession were skeptical or outraged—at displacing the hallowed stones of Greece and Rome by a vulgar industrial material. A congressman from Maryland objected on the floor of the House that while iron might make "a good dome," still nowhere did "the history of the architecture of the world present an example of an iron dome." But the newly formed American Institute of Architects heard a characteristically American defense: "It is obviously not proper or just to reject contemptuously new building materials

and new constructive devices, because they were unknown to
Phidias, to Palladio or William of Wykeham . . ."; "The cheap-
ness of iron, its rapidity and ease of workmanship . . . in the
present state of society render that metal especially precious as a
means of popular architecture."

The Congress not only approved the iron dome but was impatient for its completion. Members were persuaded by the economy and the speed with which an iron dome could be built, for
an all-stone dome would have required a whole new foundation.
Here was the opportunity, too, in a "season of universal depres-
sion in the iron trade" to provide "grateful relief to a large number of necessitous but worthy and industrious men." The new
iron dome incorporated some 9 million pounds of cast iron,
most of it cast in Brooklyn, New York, at a cost of $1,047,291.

Despite Civil War shortages of men and materials, the fifth
and final section of the bronze crowning statue of *Freedom*
(nineteen feet seven inches tall), by Thomas Crawford, was put
in place on December 2, 1863. When Crawford first submitted
his design for *Freedom* to Secretary of War Jefferson Davis in
1856, Davis requested a figure "much more vigorous," which
was duly supplied. Davis also objected to the figure's head-
dress—a "liberty cap," which he found "inappropriate to a people who were born free and would not be enslaved . . . its use, as
the badge of the freed slave." Crawford obligingly replaced the
liberty cap with "a Helmet, the crest . . . composed of an eagle's
head and a bold arrangement of feathers suggested by the cos-
tume of our Indian tribes." With a strict order against speech-
making, this statue of an armed *Freedom* triumphant in war and
peace was dedicated by a thirty-five-gun salute. The dome was
finished when Constantino Brumidi completed his *Apotheosis
of Washington* in December 1865. On the Capitol grounds we
can still enjoy the work of the greatest American landscape architect, Frederick Law Olmsted (1822–1903), who made the
grounds into a public park and embellished the setting of the

Capitol with the marble terrace to the west (1886–91) and so provided a splendid site for inaugurations.

When Walter retired in 1865, his place was taken by his assistant Edward Clark (Architect of the Capitol, 1865–1902), whose main achievement was to modernize the facilities, gradually introducing electric light in place of gas in the 1880s. But before gaslight was removed, a gas explosion in the North Wing dramatized the need to replace all remaining wooden ceilings with cast steel. The Architects after Clark—Elliott Woods (1902–1923) and David Lynn (1923–1954)—were devoted mainly to refurbishing the interior, enlarging facilities, and providing underground parking. The exterior shape of the building was modified when the East Portico was extended by thirty-three feet to provide aesthetic balance for the soaring dome, incidentally adding some ninety rooms. George M. White (1920–), as Architect of the Capitol since 1971, has taken steps to keep pace with the latest technology. Electronic voting was introduced in the House in 1973, followed by television coverage of House (1979) and Senate (1986) debates. The historic role of the Capitol was dramatized for the bicentennial celebration in 1976 by restoration of the Old Senate Chamber and the Old Supreme Court Chamber. Continuing exhibits of documents and improved interpreting services have awakened visitors to the significance of the building. The deteriorating west central front was restored by replacing its sandstone walls and reinforcing the structure with stainless-steel rods.

Our nation's Capitol expresses in some surprising ways the remarkable capacity of our New World nation to incorporate modern technology while preserving our inheritance of the best in Western culture. The capacity of the original design to be extended happily paralleled the capacity of the Federal Union to be enlarged and of the Constitution to be amended. The hope of the Framers of the Constitution for a new nation, fulfilling and exceeding Old World expectations, was expressed by Jefferson himself. In difficult times, even before there was a grand rotunda uniting the House and Senate wings, Jefferson envisaged "the first temple dedicated to the sovereignty of the people, embellishing with Athenian taste the course of a nation looking far beyond the range of Athenian destinies."

9

An Un-American Capital

Washington is a most American city, yet it is the most un-American of our cities. Created for the needs of government, it is the first modern capital created to be a national capital. Its focus and its reason for being are government. In some ways it is the most cosmopolitan of American cities, where the languages of the world can be heard on the streets and in the embassies of all nations large and small. Yet it is not an immigrant city. This is a city of contradictions. The political atmosphere of Washington is created by people who expect to stay here only temporarily, yet its culture is made by a prosperous population of people who came for one purpose and decided to stay for another. Oddly enough, the solid base of the city's population are people whose ancestors were brought here against their will. And some of the "oldest families" of the city—its black citizenry, who are the city's majority—are descendants of the forty thousand freed slaves who came and remained here after the bloody Civil War.

Though notorious for its violent crime, drugs, gangs, and teenage pregnancies, the city has a uniquely American charm. It is a city of good-humored American politics, of a richly international culture. Here we enjoy elegantly landscaped urban parks, a winding Rock Creek Parkway, open vistas, and the most richly museumed mall in the world.

The core of the city's business—its federal government buildings—is dark at night, except for the power centers. The Congress, which often meets in sessions deep into the early morning hours, keeps the lantern atop the Capitol lit, and in the White House the current resident must take calls through the night from all over the world.

Though not a culture-creating city, Washington has the richest collection of exhibits of culture—in museums of art and history and science and space and technology; the greatest and most varied library in the world, the Library of Congress; the greatest Shakespeare library in the world, the Folger Shakespeare Library; the Kennedy Center for the Performing Arts, where the world's best opera and ballet companies and symphony orchestras perform, and where some Broadway musical and dramatic successes can be seen before they go on Broadway.

Washington is a city of paradoxes. The city's slums are seldom visible to the tourist. They are not in the high-rise urban-renewal public housing tenements as they are in other cities. With a high crime rate it is the law-enforcement capital of the nation and the seat of our Supreme Court. It probably has the largest number of lawyers per capita of any city in the world, and it seems to keep most of them profitably employed.

It is a city where a million civil servants are preoccupied with bureaucratic routine, with keeping things on track, and doing a regular job, toward assured pension-security at the end. Yet the people who rule the nation from here and who give the city its special character are the president and the administration, who have a precarious tenure and must always try to look good in order to hold on for another term. The congressmen and congresswomen headquartered here are always running for office. Their roots are elsewhere (back home in the constituency), and on weekends they are only occasionally here. Their jobs depend on the opinions and whims of people hundreds or thousands of miles away. Though these Washington residents for most of their lives were rooted elsewhere, when defeated for their representative office or ousted from the executive administration they desperately seek jobs that will keep them living here—as lobby-ists, lawyers, public relations consultants, journalists, TV com-mentators, or anything else. The city's enduring cultural and commercial tone are set by the people who "stayed."

It is a city of compromise. Here you see all the artificiality of a "federal" system, where power and influence are apportioned by a rigid written scheme, yet with some of the warmth and charm of the old American South. It is a city of political syco-phancy and demagoguery and long-windedness, yet a place of frank and open political conflict, of amiable negotiation in countless committees, and of frequent noisy demonstrations by thousands of outraged protesters, persuaders, and demanders. Here there are as many fast-food counters as everywhere else, yet probably more costly expense-account restaurants per capita than anywhere else. It is a city with more than its share of dis-traught homeless, especially visible on winter streets warming over the sidewalk grates. Yet with ample institutions of compas-sion—with Gallaudet University, the nation's prime institution for the deaf, with the House of Ruth for abused women and unwed mothers, and the unexcelled National Institutes of Health. And with a magnificent interdenominational National Cathedral finally completed after eight decades. It is American, too, in the presence of competing universities, notable for their medical schools and schools of public affairs. It is a city of sur-prisingly and dismayingly few great bookstores, and yet a good public library system, and the Library of Congress.

While Washington is a city of compromises—set here between North and South as a compromise made in the 1780s between the Northern Founders and the Southern Founders of our na-tion—which conducts the nation's political business on Capitol Hill and in the White House, and even in the Supreme Court as a business of compromise, it is also a city that displays fre-quently and dramatically the nation's conflicts of views and of interests. When you walk past the White House, or up the Capi-tol's steps, you're apt to see banners and posters proclaiming some far-out demand on the president or the Congress. The messages change (and seldom are heard where it counts) but the messengers keep coming, reminding us that in this city *everybody* can say his piece, even if nobody listens.

From time to time the city is thronged with citizens from all over the nation—hordes of buses from California, Texas, Minnesota and elsewhere carrying protesters against (or for) prayer in schools, legalized abortion, nuclear armaments, subsidies to farmers, etc. If you live here you know that what people *do* here—in the White House, in Congress, in the Supreme Court— is something that people in remote corners of the country care about. This gives Washingtonians a sense of living in a center of power. It also gives all who live or work here a casual attitude toward the nation's passions and protests. They've always come, and they'll keep coming, and then they'll go away!

This is a city, too, of patriotic memories. People here have not forgotten that the British burned the Library of Congress in 1814, that the capital city was almost taken by Confederate troops in the Civil War, that it has been a wartime capital in two world wars. Patriots and heroes and veterans—even those forgotten elsewhere—are recognized in the Washington Monument, in the Jefferson Monument, in the Lincoln Memorial, in the Arlington Cemetery prominently displaying Lee's House, in the tombs of American military dead, and the Vietnam War memorial with the names of its lamented thousands.

This is a horizontal city of broad open vistas. Not here will you find the skyscraper offices and overwhelming hotel towers that are the boast of other American cities. The city is dominated by Capitol Hill, with the Congress and the Supreme Court and the Library of Congress at one end and the National Cathedral at the other. In between, instead of the checkerboard grid familiar in other nineteenth-century American cities, there is the elegant cluster-of-wheels plan of its first designer, Pierre Charles L'Enfant, with long vistas, circles, and roundabouts, and diagonal avenues named after the states. The plan still shows through, and gives the city an orderly alphabetical charm.

Though this is a cosmopolitan city, it is not a metropolis. In some ways, it is the opposite. In ancient Greece, the metropolis was the mother city. And so is London, Paris, Rome, or Lisbon. But Washington, in American upside-down fashion, is not the producer of a nation but its product, not the parent but the off-spring. From early colonial times, the Americans have had no one capital, nor do we now. This remains a federal city for a federal nation.

The transportation in and for the city also bears its mark. The timing of its Metro (underground) is governed by the needs of federal workers. It is a city with surprisingly few traffic jams, since traffic patterns are planned for the convenience of these federal workers at peak hours. The National Airport is astonishingly convenient—a fifteen-minute drive from the Congress—with reserved parking for members of Congress but, despite vast parking structures, virtually unparkable by anybody else. When you come into the city from afar, you might have landed at Dulles Airport (in Virginia) or Baltimore Washington International Airport (in Maryland), and you will discover there how the federal rivalries can actually produce a tug-of-war at the expense of ordinary citizens and tourists and how the residents are deafened by frequent jets.

The weather of the city, like its political climate, is on the whole pleasantly mild. Except for a rare bitter winter and for a few weeks of hot humid summer, the city is an outdoor delight and a gardener's paradise. Spring and fall reveal the city's special charms. The shower of white and pink cherry blossoms is sometimes late, and sometimes quickly past, but always comes. Dogwood and magnolia proclaim the spring. These times of renewal and of harvest are appropriately the city's best. Residents of the city, in their cars, can be at the ocean in an hour, or in one of the many wooded state parks in a few minutes.

And don't forget the Potomac River, still the glory of the city. In the beginning it was a main reason for putting the city here. Thomas Jefferson thought the Falls of the Potomac one of America's most attractive natural features. George Washington received his elegant London-made coach delivered to the dock of his waterfront plantation-estate at Mount Vernon, now a half-hour's drive down the river from the Capitol. Every visitor who wants to sense Washington must take the boat down the Potomac, past the fort once intended to protect the city, to grasp the reason for Washington's location.

Visitors should remember that they are viewing a peculiarly American phenomenon, the capital of a people who invented a country with a different kind of politics than is found anywhere else in the world. A federal politics, a politics without ideology, but with countless conflicting interests. This is a political capital—but only for the activities of the federal government. Residents here are only partly franchised. They can vote for president but have no voting representative in Congress. For most Americans out there away from Washington, their city government and state government are much more into their daily lives. We have fifty other political capitals.

It is no accident that this federal political capital is not a financial or a book-publishing capital, nor the artistic capital, nor the musical or dramatic capital. Washington authors are obsessively dominated by what they have experienced here, and Washington novels are the local epidemic. Unlike other national capitals, this city has no Bohemia, no Left Bank or Soho or Greenwich Village. In this democratic country, politics is something oddly apart—like this city. People come here to do their political job or to secure a favor or oppose a cause. But politics is not this nation's main stream.

The historical paradox of the city is expressed in the city itself. In a nation where blacks are only a minority, the federal capital is governed by blacks. But they play a small role in the cultural life of the city.

While Washington is not a culture-producing capital, it is a culture-displaying capital, perhaps one of the grandest, but surely the most focused, in the world. And in the last twenty years it has become more so than ever. Nowhere else in the world is there a mall with so full an assortment of museums exhibiting the world's nature and the world's cultures. The Smithsonian Institution has refurbished the National Museum of American Art, the National Portrait Gallery, has built the National Museum of American History, the Hirshhorn Museum and Sculpture Garden, the Air and Space Museum, the Freer Gallery of Eastern Art, and the Museums of African Art and Near Eastern Culture. The National Gallery of Art houses one of the world's great collections. The Corcoran Gallery and the Phillips Collection offer uniquely important art treasures. The Library of Congress, the most cosmopolitan and diversified library in the world, includes a third building named after President Madison, the largest public building in Washington, symbolic of this free country's New World way of including the world and reaching out to the world. This is the capital of a nation whose mission is a bringing together. And anyone who comes here from anywhere can easily become an American by staying and joining in the quest.

IV

THE CAUTIONARY
SCIENCE

*A large acquaintance with particulars
often makes us wiser than the possession
of abstract formulas, however deep.*

—William James,
The Varieties of Religious Experience

10

Tocqueville's America

The most interesting question for the newcomer to *Democracy in America,* by Alexis de Tocqueville (1805–59), is why this book, of all the myriad travel accounts of the United States, should have become the classic—the standard source for generalizing about America. From Tocqueville's own era, two best-selling books on the United States—Mrs. Trollope's *Domestic Manners of the Americans* (1832) and Charles Dickens's *American Notes* (1842)—by more clever stylists and more experienced observers than Tocqueville, survive only as scholarly footnotes. They tell us about those curious earlier Americans, but Tocqueville tells us about ourselves. He speaks to us every day. The others amuse us by anecdotes and strictures on contemporary American manners and morals. But Tocqueville, like other classics of political thought, has the ring of prophecy. For him America was both the enticing object and the universal symbol of a New World in the making. He was a master at seeing and describing the symbolism. Even more important, he wrote with an uncanny feeling for the grand currents of history and with a wholesome sense of how much and how little we can deflect those currents.

For Tocqueville history was a cautionary science. This was his way of alerting his own and later generations to the risks that would come with the promise of our New World. The first part of *Democracy in America* put in historical and geographic perspective the origins and character of American laws, constitutions, and politics, including the influence of religion, the role of majorities, and the significance of a nation of three races. The second part, taking off from the American experience to observations about the world, assessed the influence of equality on thought and feeling, on art, literature, morals, and the relations of the sexes, and the special perils threatening democratic societies.

Democracy in America was itself a minor literary miracle, reminding us to be cautious before we generalize about the paths to profound insights into ourselves and our institutions. A young aristocrat of twenty-six, with little experience of politics or the world, Tocqueville spent only nine months (May 11, 1831, to February 20, 1832) in the United States. He came here at his family's expense to escape the kaleidoscopic confusion of French politics, and for the limited purpose of studying the American penal system. He had the companionship of another young aristocrat, Gustave de Beaumont, but of course none of the apparatus or assistance that modern social scientists take for granted. He had no team of interviewers, no quantifying devices. He did take notes, which he organized and indexed under sixty-four headings when he returned to Paris. And he read intensely in a few American legal classics. He had been deeply influenced by the historian François Guizot's prophecy of the decline of aristocracy and was a close student of English parliamentary history. Eighteen months after his return he retreated to an attic room in his family's house at 49, rue de Verneuil. There, in less than a year he completed Part I of *Democracy* (published in January 1835), which brought him fame at the age of thirty. Four years later he produced Part II, published in April 1840.

Tocqueville's distinctive message and the unique appeal of his book came from the fact that he was not merely an alert traveler, an acute student of politics and society. His book endures because he had the vision of a historian for the history-making events of his time, which still leave their mark on ours.

Family memories had made it impossible for him to forget that he was living in an era of French revolutions. His great-grandfather Chrétien de Malesherbes, an eminent liberal reformer and friend of the *Encyclopédistes,* had been banished by Louis XV, recalled by Louis XVI, whom the revolutionaries allowed him to defend, and then guillotined (along with his daughter and grandchildren) in 1794. The "de" in his name was supplied in 1827, when the Bourbon king Charles X made his father a peer. Tocqueville himself had been made an apprentice magistrate. But when the "Citizen King," Louis Phillipe of Orléans, came to power in July 1830, Tocqueville's family was suspect for its Bourbon loyalties. Tocqueville saw France tumbling toward the social equality that he thought was already realized in America, especially since the rise of Andrew Jackson.

Tocqueville, though no romantic, shared Wordsworth's delight at being alive and young in that dawning age of revolution. But, not being a poet, his celebration would take the form of a long prose epic on the meaning of the new age in the New World. "I am firmly convinced," he said, "that the democratic revolution which we are now beholding is an irresistible fact, against which it would be neither desirable nor prudent to contend." On the way back from America he and Beaumont visited England (August 3 to September 7, 1832) to see firsthand the heritage of "John Bull, Father of Jonathan (America)," and incidentally see his English fiancée and meet her family. "They say that [the English] are definitely on the edge of revolution and that one should hurry over to see them as they are now! I am therefore making haste to go to England as though it were the last performance of a fine play." In England, then in travail over the first Reform Bill (not passed until December 1832), he observed still another way of moving from aristocracy to democracy.

He had an acute vision for the common denominator of the history of his time. Young and still politically uncommitted, with nothing but a minor magistracy to lose, he wrote not as an advocate or polemicist but as a historian of the long term. "The development of the principle of equality" is "a providential fact. . . . it is universal, it is lasting, it constantly eludes all human interference, and all events as well as all men contribute to its progress." The purpose of his book, he said, was "to show what a democratic people really was in our day . . . by a rigorously accurate picture." Fifteen years later, in 1848, he could declare that his historical intuitions had already been confirmed by "the advent of democracy as a governing power in the world's affairs, universal and irresistible."

Luckily, when Tocqueville wrote his *Democracy in America,* he was still young enough not to have hostages to political fortune, and was painfully aware of the volatility of French politics. So he felt freer than established writers or politicians to assess the price and the rewards of the new society he saw emerging. "Though a republic may develop less than other governments of the noblest powers of the human mind, it yet has a nobility of its own."

Tocqueville's twin purposes were to awaken his contemporaries to the "providential" currents of equality that they could only vainly try to obstruct, and at the same time to awaken the beneficiaries of the new currents to impending dangers. His book was to be as much about the threat of the tyranny of the majority as about the promise of equality. Nowhere are his prophecies more poignant. In the worlds of thought and feeling, he announced, democracy itself had created a new tyrant—Public Opinion. The apparently "mixed" nature of our political institutions was misleading. And long before opinion polls or best-seller statistics, Tocqueville saw the powers of this strange new democratic monster. "The majority lives in the perpetual utterance of self-applause, and there are certain truths which the Americans can learn only from strangers or from experience."

And what does this mean for the thinking, feeling individual, always his focus? "Whenever social conditions are equal, public opinion presses with enormous weight upon the minds of each individual: it surrounds, directs, and oppresses him. . . . As men grow more alike, each man feels himself weaker in regard to all the rest. . . . he mistrusts himself as soon as they assail him." We Americans, then, have a special need for our Tocquevilles.

For us, much of the charm and wisdom of *Democracy in America* comes from Tocqueville's skill in the cautionary science. "The nations of our time cannot prevent the condition of men from becoming equal, but it depends upon themselves whether the principle of equality is to lead them to servitude or freedom, to knowledge or barbarism, to prosperity or wretchedness." Without denying the force of the great historic movement he was witnessing, he gives us a sense that each of us still is not without a role in history. It is more urgent than ever that we take personal control of our own thought and feeling. By focusing on this congenital menace of democracy he reassures us that each of us has a secret private power to resist the unseen tyrant. We can and must find counterbalancing opportunities for art and expression. If we read and heed Tocqueville's cautions, in our time we will not be whistling in the dark.

It would be easy to survey the weaknesses of contemporary American society in the chapter headings of Part II of *Democracy*. Long before the age of book publishing and "entertainment" conglomerates, Tocqueville warned that "Democracy not only infuses a taste for letters among the trading classes, but introduces a trading spirit into literature." With the now familiar result. "The ever increasing crowd of readers," he prophesied, "and their continuing craving for something new ensure the sale of books that nobody much esteems." And he reminds us that the study of Greek and Latin is peculiarly useful in democratic communities. "All who would aspire to literary excellence in democratic nations ought frequently to refresh themselves at the springs of ancient literature; there is no more wholesome medicine for the mind. . . . they have some special merits admirably calculated to counterbalance our peculiar defects. They are a prop on the side to which we are in most danger of falling." His book overflows with unfamiliar wisdom that touches our everyday America.

Although Tocqueville writes about a nation and a continent, his overwhelming concern is for the individual. Haunted by a well-documented fear of the powers of democracy to frighten and submerge the individual, he was a prophet—even an inventor—of individualism. The very word "individualism" first entered our English language in 1840 through Henry Reeve's translation of Part II of Tocqueville's *Democracy in America*. "Individualism," Tocqueville observed, "is a novel expression, to which a novel idea has given birth. . . . Individualism is a mature and calm feeling, which disposes each member of the community to sever himself from the mass of his fellow-creatures, and to draw apart with his family and friends." For him, oddly enough, individualism seemed an antidote to the congenital ills of equality in a democratic society. And in his focus on the self, Tocqueville was prophetic not only of American society but of the future of Western art and literature in which America would be a leader.

The enduring popularity of Tocqueville's book is itself an omen of the vitality of democracy in America. For it shows our willingness to listen to critical alien voices, young or old, whoever they may be and wherever they come from. They prevent our being embarrassed by the thought that we may be the hope of the world, and they help us see the perils in our prosperity. "Men will not receive the truth from their enemies," Tocqueville reminded us, "and it is very seldom offered to them by their friends; on this account I have frankly uttered it."

11

Custine's Russia

The lively travel classic *Empire of the Czar* (translated from *La Russie en 1839*), by the Marquis de Custine (1790–1857), can help Western readers discover what Russia really was and help us ask whether that Russia is still there. In the mid-nineteenth century the eminent Russian socialist author Alexandr Herzen said this was the best book ever written by a foreigner about Russia. Today, George Kennan contends that while perhaps this may not be a very good book about Russia in 1839, it is an excellent book about the Russia of Joseph Stalin and not a bad book about the Russia of Brezhnev and Kosygin. Custine's prophetic insights can help us grasp the problems faced by anyone who tries to bring change to the Empire of the Czar.

Besides being a vivid account of horse-drawn travels in an exotic land, this is an uncanny and tantalizing book. "It is true I have not fully seen," wrote Custine, "but I have fully divined." What gives any man the clairvoyant power to divine the broad deep currents of a nation's life? This question becomes more interesting as we read Custine. Although he was in Russia for less than three months he showed that power. He somehow sensed features of Russian life and institutions that reached back for millennia before his time and would extend forward for more than a century. Following the daily adventures of this witty, penetrating, but passionate and prejudiced observer, we are constantly amazed that his breadth of insight could so far exceed the scope of his observations. And we are tantalized by the thought that though some of his facts may be inaccurate or exaggerated or maliciously distorted, many of his conclusions still survive at this distance of time.

To be fair to Custine we must first of all travel along with him, sharing the adventures and misadventures into which his aggressive curiosity and hypersensitivity led him. Few of us would have chosen him for a traveling companion. He did not have the good fortune of Tocqueville, who, about the same time, was making the brief trip to the United States that produced his classic *Democracy in America* and had the companionship of an amiable and intimate friend and collaborator, Gustave de Beaumont. Tocqueville's observations would have the benefit of being tested by the sobering criticisms of this alter ego. But Custine was a loner. As George Kennan explains, Custine's sensitivities had been sharpened by a life of personal tragedy, and his hypersensitivity had been cultivated by incidents that had made him the most notorious homosexual in Paris and caused his ostracism from the polite literary society where he belonged. What we have from Custine, then, are his extremely personal, untempered, and frequently intemperate opinions, based on the experiences that he describes in unforgettable detail.

Custine had the insights of an outsider. Even without drawing any subtle conclusions from these episodes, we can enjoy the variety, the color, and the semi-Asiatic strangeness of Russia a century and a half ago that he depicts with eloquence. We join the fetes and royal weddings in St. Petersburg, we share his delight in the river-broken vistas of the city, we listen in on his conversations with the "truly Russian" Czar Nicholas I and the affable Czarina and share his ambivalent admiration of the Autocrat of all the Russias. We jog and jiggle along in rickety carriages on rough roads, with the daily threat of being stuck up to our axles in mud. We overnight in flea-bitten inns. We share the warmth and festivity of country-fair music and dance, and we admire the rounded beauty of the peasant women. We sense the urban provincialism of Yaroslav and Nijni Novgorod, and become familiar with the Volga boatmen. We are dazzled by the Oriental splendor of the Kremlin, day and night.

None of this calls for an elaborate ideological gloss. But we are soon struck, and sometimes dumbfounded, by the prophetic accuracy of some of his observations—beginning with the bureaucratic hassle at the border on the way in. We share Custine's irritation at the sullen police spy who has been assigned to him as a servant and whom he cannot shake off. His portrait of the grim prison at Schlüsselburg, of meaningless interrogations, of incarceration for indefinable crimes, of the pain of exiles to Siberia, seems all too familiar. He describes poignantly the miseries visited on the children of convicts, the omnipresence of secrecy and suspicion. His anecdotes make us wonder how much of the eternal Russia is still there. He gives us a discomfiting feeling of déjà vu.

As a venture into the world of political speculation, Custine's journey to Russia was a counterpart of Tocqueville's nine-month voyage to America. Tocqueville, the young liberal aristocrat witnessing the decline of aristocracy and the rise of equality at home in France, went with Beaumont to learn what he could from America. And the first part of his *Democracy in America* would depict the great opportunities (and new risks) of an egalitarian society in a new world. The Marquis de Custine was haunted by the memory of his father and grandfather, whose guillotining by the French revolutionaries he painfully recounts. He went to Russia to document the advantages of autocracy and confirm his prejudices against popular government. But it was there that he discovered the evils of autocracy, and he returned to France a strong advocate of constitutions.

Custine's conclusions are sometimes surprising, but always interesting to an American democrat. For example, he was a firm believer in the social advantages of a true aristocracy—a class of people who were equipped, qualified, and trained to preserve liberties against a despot. He saw such a class in England. But in Russia, surprisingly, he found no aristocracy. For there all classes, including the "noblemen," were equally slaves of the autocrat Czar. Russian courtiers did not deserve to be dignified as aristocrats because they were nothing but fawning syco- phants. He was appalled at this "moral degradation of the higher classes." The Empire of the Czar, according to him, was already a truly "classless" society. Below the autocrat himself there were no grades of independence or dignity, but a whole nation of fear-struck slaves.

Some will say that today, when men of goodwill are trying to bring us together with the Russians, is no time to remind us of the deep currents of Russian history that separate them from us—the Mongolian invasions, the recurrent fears of attacks from the West, the unbroken traditions of autocracy and se- crecy, and the absence of any tradition of constitutions, of a legally authorized opposition, of private rights of expression, or free worship and free emigration.

No two nations are more urgently in need of understanding each other. What this book can do is to encourage realistic hopes and discourage utopian expectations.

Custine can help us correct the modern myopia. His spirited and readable narrative can remind us that beneath the veil of the USSR there always remained Russia—a legacy of the Empire of the Czar. No more than others can the Russian people escape their history. We would have understood the Soviets far better if we had more vividly remembered the history of their institutions, their ways of life, and their rulers. Those were the makings of the Empire of the Czar, and are the makings too of Russia today.

History can bring charity to our judgment of the Russians, and patience to our expectations of their treatment of their citi- zens. Perhaps, then, we will not blame them so blatantly for so long refusing to grant what their history and institutions make difficult or impossible for them (e.g., free emigration, free press, free speech, freedom of religion, an opposition party). The Russians can no more forget the centuries of Mongolian occupation, the traditions of expansion across Europe and Asia, the sacredness of Czarist autocracy, the identity of state religion, the traditions of secrecy and police tyranny, of knouting and Siberian exile, than Americans can forget the millennium of Magna Carta tradition, of parliaments, bills of rights, constitutions, habeas corpus, common-law judges, free land, copious immigration, a moving frontier, and a bloody civil war. We will have greater sympathy for and patience for Russian efforts to inch away from the institutions that Custine describes in his *Empire of the Czar.*

New England Puritans of our colonial age could never be *disillusioned,* simply because they were never illusioned. Their concept of Original Sin made them surprised and grateful that corrupt man could accomplish anything. Similarly, a sense of history can rescue us, too, from extravagant optimism and painful disappointments about Russian gropings to escape the ways of life described in this book.

Custine, depicting the grandeur and color as well as the backwardness of the Russian empire in the nineteenth century, can remind us that some tendencies that we have attributed to "Communism" may simply be Russian: expansionism, autocracy, bureaucracy, centralism, secrecy, contempt for personal rights and public opinion, etc. In all these ways Custine can help us to a deeper, more charitable understanding.

This book is a brilliant example of an ancient genre, as old as Herodotus, that brings together the arts of literature and the techniques of social science to enrich our understanding of our fellow human beings. From the very beginning of Western culture, travelers and traveler-historians have put flesh and blood on the fearful abstractions of politics. After reading Custine's account of his conversations with Nicholas I, we have a more intimate view of the autocrat's problems, his strengths and weaknesses. We can plainly see that the Czar, too, was only another man. While Custine may make us more wary of Russians as political animals, he also makes us more sympathetic to them as human beings. I know of no other book that more vividly and suspensefully uses travel narrative to sketch institutions. The bizarre personality of the author, his uncompromising prejudices and passions, and the uncertain authenticity of particular facts simply add interest. Every reader is challenged by one of the more acute and eloquent travelers of the last century.

The American reader may also find Custine his guide to rediscovering America. The astonishing symmetry—Hegel would have called it "antithesis"—between the history of Russia and the history of the United States has often been noticed. It was in the mind of Tocqueville himself as he concluded the book that made him famous. The first volume of his *Democracy in America* ends with these prophetic words:

> the Russians and the Americans . . . have suddenly placed themselves in the front rank among the nations, and the world learned their existence and their greatness at almost the same time.
> All other nations seem to have nearly reached their natural limits, and they have only to maintain their power; but these are still in the act of growing. All the others have stopped, or continue to advance with extreme difficulty; these alone are proceeding with ease and celerity along a path to which no limit can be perceived. The American struggles against the obstacles that nature imposes on him; the adversaries of the Russians are men. The former combats the wilderness and savage life; the latter, civilization with all its arms. The conquests of the American are therefore gained by the plowshare; those of the Russian by the sword. The Anglo-American relies upon personal interest to accomplish his ends and gives free scope to the unguided strength and common sense of the people; the Russian centers all authority of society in a single arm. The principal instrument of the former is freedom; of the latter, servitude. Their starting-point is different and their courses are not the same; yet each of them seems marked out by the will of Heaven to sway the destinies of half the globe.

Tocqueville was not far wrong.

Where are there better examples of the contrasting possibilities of history and civilization on this planet? A cosmic Plutarch writing the *Parallel Lives of Great Nations* could not find a more rewarding subject. Perhaps it could be called *Mark Twain or Dostoevsky?*

Custine's vivid overstatements of the features of Russian history throw the large contours of American history into bold relief. At his entrance through the port of Kronstadt, "ice-locked during six months of the year" and with the "simple formalities" of the customs police in St. Petersburg, the miasma of fear and suspicion of all foreigners arises and is never dispelled. To the question "What is your object in Russia?" Custine responds, "To see the country." To which the officer objects, " 'That is not here a motive for travelling!' (What humility in this objection!)" Custine repeatedly reminds us that the Russian fear of foreigners and obsession with government secrecy is no whim of bureaucrats but the understandable reaction to centuries of rule by Mongolian invaders, repeated later invasions and threats of invasion, and landlocked isolation. Lacking year-round seaborne access to the Western world, menaced by continent-spanning land borders, what more natural than that the Russian of 1839 should view foreigners with suspicion? Who but an invader or his agent would come "to see the country"?

All this had enduring consequences for Russia's diplomatic relations:

> Let but the liberty of the press be accorded to Russia for twenty-four hours, and we should learn things that would make us recoil with horror. Silence is indispensible to oppression. Under an absolute government every indiscretion of speech is equivalent to a crime of high treason.
>
> If there are found among Russians better diplomatists than among nations the most advanced in civilisation, it is because our journals inform them of every thing which is done or projected among ourselves, and because, instead of prudently disguising our weaknesses, we display them, with passion, every morning; whilst, on the contrary, the Byzantine policy of the Russians, working in the

dark, carefully conceals from us everything that is thought, done, or feared among them. We march exposed on all sides, they advance under cover. The ignorance in which they leave us blinds our view; our sincerity enlightens theirs; we suffer from all the evils of idle talking, they have the advantages of secrecy; and herein lies all their skill and ability.

The reader must be constantly cautioned and reminded that the land he is traveling is the Russia of 1839, a century and a half ago. Obviously we cannot understand any nation, including our own, without knowing its past. And especially in the case of Russia we need every kind of help that can be found toward a fuller knowledge of that past. For in recent decades the Russians—even after becoming Soviets—have not given themselves or us much reliable help. When Custine reports the words of the Russian nobleman Prince K., he describes this problem:

> Russian despotism not only pays little respect to ideas and sentiments, it will also deny facts; it will struggle against evidence, and triumph in the struggle!!! for evidence, when it is inconvenient to power, has no more voice among us than has justice. . . . The people, and even the great men, are resigned spectators of this war against truth; the lies of the despot, however palpable, are always flattering to the slave. . . . in Russia . . . despotism is more powerful than nature; the emperor is not only the representative of God, he is himself the creative power: a power greater than that of Deity, for it only extends its action to the future, whereas the emperor alters and amends the past: the law has no retroactive effect, the caprice of a despot has.

Which makes the republication of Custine's travels and the reports of other outsiders all the more welcome.

On its first appearance in French and English in 1843 this book sold widely. Custine claimed a sale of some two hundred thousand copies within three years, which was enormous in those days. This could hardly have been the result of the reviews. Such French reviews as appeared were predominantly unfavorable, some of them savage. Custine wittily attributed the large sale of the first printing to the fact that the leading Paris editors had ignored the book. In England also the major reviews were unfavorable. The poet-politician Richard Monckton Milnes, not entirely unfairly, called Custine "a theorist and generalizer of the wildest character." "He is sincere, although his sincerity may not be of the purest stamp—he is earnest, though his earnestness may be affected by self-conceit—he is fair, in so far as fairness consists in giving us the separate impressions, as they successively passed across his mind." When *Empire of the Czar* first appeared in English, it was ignored in the United States. Of course the book was banned in Russia, where even discussion of it was forbidden.

It is not surprising that the book aroused passions when it first appeared, as it will perhaps now once again. For it is a delectable mixture, in George Kennan's phrase, of "things sufficiently inaccurate to be annoying (mostly matters of detailed fact) and ones that were sufficiently true to hurt." If the book was never a *succès d'estime,* it has the distinction nevertheless of being a *succès d'histoire.* The reader today will be grateful to the unhappy marquis for having made his journey and for having left this unvarnished record. Which gives us all a much-needed incentive and opportunity, with the aid of Custine's acute eye and acerbic pen, to speculate on the relation between Russia's past and its present.

Despite its shortcomings and distortions, and Soviet efforts to pretend that the book never existed, the book lives on—an antique mirror in which to see one of the most mysterious nations of our time. Custine himself finally saw his book as just that—a mirror for himself and for us. He concluded:

> If ever your sons should be discontented with France, try my receipt; tell them to go to Russia. It is a useful journey for every foreigner: whoever has well examined that country will be content to live any-

where else. It is always well to know that a society exists where no happiness is possible, because by a law of his nature, man cannot be happy unless he is free.

Such a recollection renders the traveller less fastidious; and, returning to his own hearth, he can say of his country what a man of mind once said of himself: "When I estimate myself, I am modest; but when I compare myself, I am proud."

THE FOURTH KINGDOM

"Pass in, pass in," the angels say,
"In to the upper doors,
Nor count compartments of the floors,
But mount to paradise
By the stairway of surprise."

—Ralph Waldo Emerson, *Merlin*

12

Darwinian Expectations

*Darwin has interested us in the history of
nature's technology.*
—Karl Marx, *Capital* (1867)

We live in an age of prophecy. Much of what passes for news in the United States today is somebody's latest view of what the future will bring. Much of what passes for history is a description in the past tense of the ghosts of the future. The memories of the New Deal and FDR, the shadows of JFK and the Bay of Pigs, the Cold War, the war in Vietnam, and the Gulf War, are fashioned into stencils for the future. From the very beginning, the settlement of our so-called New World was overcast with futuristic enthusiasms. Without a known past, America had to be called the Land of the Future.

But prophecy is not what it used to be. In Western civilization, in the Judeo-Christian tradition, the original and primary meaning of "prophet" was quite different from what it is now. The earliest meaning of the word in English, as the *Oxford English Dictionary* tells us, is "One who speaks for God or for any deity, as the inspired revealer or interpreter of his will; one who is held or (more loosely) who claims to have this function; an inspired, or quasi-inspired teacher." The English word is derived from Greek words that meant to speak forth or to speak for another.

In ancient Greece the prophet was the interpreter of a divinity, such as Zeus, Dionysus, or Apollo, or the deliverer of an oracle, in Latin known as *vates*. In the West we owe the first and most powerful definition of our prophetic tradition to the Hebrew prophets, who constitute the second division of the Hebrew Canon (Law, Prophets, Writings). The great Hebrew prophetic movement, which, after Amos, c. 750 B.C., lasted at least half a millennium, is credited by religious historians as the main force that gave Israel its spiritual stature and influence. This tradition was, of course, carried on (and, Christians would say, fulfilled) in the New Testament prophets, or the apostles. Luke believed that from the beginning of the world, God had been speaking by "the mouth of his holy prophets" (1:70). "Prophecy came not in old time by the will of man," said Peter, "but holy men of God spake as they were moved by the Holy Ghost" (II Pet. 1:21). And the power of the tradition was affirmed anew in Islam, where the messiah was clearly and simply designated as The Prophet.

The Hebrew prophets were often doomsayers, forecasting the disasters that would be God's punishment for the obstinate evils of the present generation. They were more important as preachers than as forecasters. They pleaded for righteousness, mercy, justice, and love of God. "Seek good, and not evil, that ye may live:" exhorted Amos, "and so the Lord, the God of hosts, shall be with you" (Amos: 5:14). The prophets dared to castigate the rich and the powerful precisely because they considered themselves messengers of the highest power, somehow sharing in the mysteries of the universe.

This apostolic role of the prophet, as messenger of doom and divine retribution, has gradually been displaced from our everyday usage by a more secular, naturalistic sense. For us the prophet is a forecaster of morally neutral events. Thus we speak of a weather prophet or a financial prophet, or forecasters of shifts in public opinion or of voting behavior. This change in usage and emphasis has come with the rise of modern science. By 1736 Bishop Joseph Butler was writing in his *Analogy of the*

Christian Religion that "Prophecy is nothing but the history of events before they come to pass."

Just as the prophet played a moral, homiletic role, so too would the "natural philosopher," the student of natural history. While the theologian aimed to "vindicate the ways of God to man," the pious observer of nature aimed to justify the ways of God in the whole Creation. According to the Book of Genesis, on the third day, God created vegetation—grass, herbs, and fruit, each reproducing after its kind. Then, on the fifth day, God began to create animals—first fishes and birds, then land animals and finally man (sixth day), each designed to reproduce after its kind. These two realms of nature came to be called the animal kingdom and the vegetable kingdom. With modern chemistry and physics and the discovery of their special laws, people in the West began to speak of a third, or a mineral, kingdom. One of the first to use this expression in English was the great Robert Boyle (1627–1691), discoverer of Boyle's Law— that at a constant temperature the volume of a gas is inversely proportionate to the pressure. As Boyle himself noted, this way of speaking came with the rising chemistry and physics in his own time. Boyle, who insisted that the study of nature was a religious duty, set the natural philosopher the task of discovering the laws by which the physical world functioned, and which kept God's whole Creation in working order. In the West the three Kingdoms—animal, vegetable, and mineral—became a proverbial way of describing exhaustively the whole range of natural bodies.

"Natural philosophers" described the relations among the animal kingdom, the vegetable kingdom, and the mineral kingdom and the relations among all creatures by a divinely ordered scheme, "the economy of nature." This husbanding of divine creative energy was eloquently summarized by Joseph Priestley (1733–1804), the English clergyman-chemist, discoverer of oxygen, and friend of Thomas Jefferson:

The clouds and the rain are designed to moisten the earth, and the sun to warm it; and the texture and juices of the earth are formed so as to receive the genial influences of both, in order to ripen and bring to perfection that infinite variety of plants and fruits, the seeds of which are deposited in it. Again, is not each plant peculiarly adapted to its proper soil and climate, so that every country is furnished with those productions which are peculiarly suited to it? Are not all plants likewise suited to the various kinds of animals which feed upon them? . . . The various kinds of animals are, again, in a thousand ways adapted to, and formed for, the use of one another. Beasts of a fiercer nature prey upon the tamer cattle: fishes of a larger size live almost wholly upon those of a less: and there are some birds which prey upon land animals, others upon fishes, and others upon creatures of their own species.

(*Discourses on Various Subjects*, Birmingham, 1787, p. 303)

This was the dynamic of nature, but there was also an order in nature's very structure.

The ruling metaphor for this structure, a counterpart to the economy of nature, was the Great Chain of Being. This was the simple and vivid notion that all the species of plants and animals could be ranged in a neat and orderly chain from the lowliest insect or worm up through the more complicated animals to man himself, who was only a little lower than the angels. In the familiar couplets by Alexander Pope (1688–1744):

> Vast chain of being! which from God
>   began,
> Natures aethereal, human, angel, man,
> Beast, bird, fish, insect, what no eye can see,
> No glass can reach; from Infinite to thee,
> From thee to nothing.—On superior pow'rs
> Were we to press, inferior might on ours;
> Or in the full creation leave a void,
> Where, one step broken, the great scale's
>   destroy'd;
> From Nature's chain whatever link you
>   strike,
> tenth, or ten thousandth, breaks the chain
>   alike.

The chain of being was another name for God's plenitude. The earth could not be more full than it was. This seemed to mean also that in the beginning God had created every possible species, that none could become obsolete, and none ever be added. Toward the goal, in the words of the Psalmist, that "the whole earth be filled with his glory" (Psalm 72:19). So the great Linnaeus could describe and taxonomize a *Systema Naturae,* a System of Nature.

All these were commonplaces of Western thought at the end of the eighteenth century. When Charles Darwin published his *Origin of Species* in England in 1859, he made a momentous revision and adaptation of this traditional vocabulary to an age when the pace of change was accelerating, when the status of men and women seemed newly fluid, when institutions were in flux, and even academics were recognizing change as a fact of life.

The full-fledged Darwinian theory of evolution was fed by springs and currents from the ancient Greeks, by Saint Augustine's suggestions that God had actually provided some seeds in the beginning that would not sprout until later times, by medieval notions of an organic world, by the hints of French philosophers and naturalists (Montesquieu, Diderot, Buffon, and others), and even by the doubts of the absolute fixity of species harbored by Linnaeus, the high priest of traditional taxonomy. Charles's own grandfather, Erasmus Darwin, wrote an epic on the urges of plants and animals to develop new forms. And we must not forget, too, that Charles Darwin was not alone in his day, for Alfred Russel Wallace quite independently on the other side of the globe had arrived at the same notions, even using substantially the same vocabulary. All this suggests that Darwinism was not so much a revolution as a climax. Among the clues to its providential fitness for the new age of accelerated change was the transformation of the word and idea of "Revolution," which came about the same time. "Revolution," which had once meant simply another return of a cycle (like the reproduction of species after its kind), now had a new meaning. The world's great age would begin anew.

Of all the ironies of intellectual history, none is more surprising, then, than that Darwin's work should have been called "revolutionary." In fact it was less the harbinger of a new age than a summing up and revision of accepted ways of thinking. The economy of nature was now restated as the idea of natural selection and the survival of the fittest. Instead of an abstract chain of being there was now a copiously populated environment, with every niche filled by an organism peculiarly and competitively adapted to it. The idea of species—with each "reproducing after its kind"—remained central, but the machinery for creating species was modified, and the possibility of the extinction of species became conceivable. The climactic nature of Darwin's thought was revealed in the fact that the initial shock of orthodox churchmen at his revision of the Book of Genesis was so soon transformed into a general acclaim by the literate scientific and literary community. "The Abraham of science," John Tyndall applauded in 1871, "—a searcher as obedient to the command of truth as was the patriarch to the command of God." Upon his death in 1882 Darwin was buried with all religious rites in Westminster Abbey.

The religious roots of Darwin's works are well known and widely acknowledged. His family intended him for the clergy from an early age. To persuade Darwin's father that the twenty-two-year-old Charles be allowed to go off as a naturalist companion to the captain on the voyage of the *Beagle,* his uncle Josiah Wedgwood II had to argue, "The pursuit of Natural History, though certainly not professional, is very suitable to a clergyman." Although in later years Darwin had increasing doubts about dogmatic religion, he remained sensitive and responsive to the religious sentiments of his pious family. We have often heard how, when Karl Marx expressed his desire to dedicate Volume One of the English translation of *Das Kapital* to Darwin, he demurred. It would pain his family, Charles insisted, to see dedicated to him a work so godless.

We inherit the dominant ideas in our thinking about the future from the natural historians, from the writers on the economy of nature and their evolutionary successors who attained classic expression in the writing of Darwin and his followers. They reflected on and classified the objects found in the three great kingdoms—animal, vegetable, and mineral. Their axioms came from the age of biology, when most of the peoples of Western Europe and America were living on farms, and when their livelihood depended on the products of nature.

These have had the power of "vested ideas"—ideas so familiar that we have ceased to be aware that we live with them. "Vested" has just the right overtones, for "to vest" is related to an old German word that means "to wear" (as in vestment, a man's vest, etc.). We forget about these six ideas just as we forget the clothes we are wearing provided they fit, that is, provided they conform to us in a familiar and comfortable and fashionable way.

Dualism. This was belief in a simple antithesis between the organism on the one hand and the conditions of its life on the other—between the pond where the ducks lived and the various species of ducks that struggled to survive in the pond. The duck that won the struggle was one whose webfeet and mode of flight suited it best for its surroundings. Out of this axiom came the idea of "environment." The word "environ" first came into English (c. 1400) to mean "to form a ring around, surround, encircle," and "environment" originally meant the act of environing. Only in the nineteenth century, in the lifetime of Darwin, did the word take on the now-common concrete sense—"that which environs," or the surroundings. This made the word specific and useful for biology, and incidentally froze it, helping to freeze much of our social thinking into the dualist mode. "The organism," it could now be said, "is continually adapting to its environment." Of course there were a few kinds of organisms—such as the coral with its coral reefs or the ant in its large anthills—that were conspicuously creating their own environment. These cases especially interested Darwin, as did the domesticated animals, perhaps because they all suggested subtleties in the very notion of environment. But Darwin kept his spotlight on natural selection, which tested the ability of a plant or an animal to survive in a given environment. The environment was the scene within which the different species did battle, the circumstances that set the conditions and the stakes of the struggle, modified only, if at all, by the slow processes of climate and geology. The winner was the one best suited to play a role on that stage.

Conflict. Any plant or animal emerged victorious on the environmental scene only after winning against adversaries, a struggle for survival. In Tennyson's words the world of evolution was "Nature, red in tooth and claw." *The Origin of Species* might well have been called a chronicle of the conflict of species or the extinction of species. As Priestley and other philosophers of the economy of nature had observed, all creatures lived by preying on other creatures. Nature was a scene of blood and death, where evolutionary thinkers described the process of a progressive and uplifting purpose. The carnage spelled progress, signaling the emergence of new and always better-adapted species.

Hierarchy. What was produced was a scale in nature from the simplest to the most complex. While the older tradition of natural history described this hierarchy as the Great Chain of Being, the newer tradition, classically applied to society by Herbert Spencer, affirmed, "Progress . . . is not an accident, but a necessity. . . . It is a part of nature." In his *Principles of Biology* (1864) he coined the phrase "survival of the fittest," which suggested that, like all nature, the evolution of society and culture revealed a predetermined movement from an incoherent homogeneity to a complex and interdependent heterogeneity. What the earlier natural philosophers saw as a ladder of Creation in space, created in the beginning by God, later natural philosophers saw God creating in time by the inevitable processes of evolution.

Displacement. This meant, of course, the displacement of earlier, more primitive forms by later, more complex, more subtly adapted forms. The cumbersome pterodons of the late Cretaceous period in Europe, Asia, and North America (some with a wingspan of twenty-five feet), lacked feathers and did not have a keel bone at the breast to which the powerful flight muscles of birds might have been attached. So of course they inevitably gave way to the birds, so much better adapted to fill the ecological niche. The Darwinian history of nature was a story of slow but constant and inevitable elbowing out of the less well adapted by the better-adapted species. In the long run, nature simply would not tolerate the survival of creatures not economically adapted to their environment.

Response. All of this development was possible because the life and destiny of plants and animals was a story of response to a fixed set of "needs." These needs of plants or animals varied of course from species to species, but for any species they were constant. Each branch of the animal kingdom had needs that could be satisfied only by the conditions of its appropriate environment. Thus the creatures of the foreshore thrived in the tidal ebb and flow, and the bills and feet of shorebirds were adapted for retrieving their food from the sand. Every environment was suited to satisfy certain needs and not others. Naturalists observing what Lawrence Henderson called "The Fitness of the Environment" noted the suitability of the ocean waters—their salinity and temperature—for sustaining the fish and plants that flourished there. Historians, too, have followed these clues. Arnold Toynbee built a whole theory of the rise and fall of civilizations on a notion of "challenge" and "response." The fixed set of challenges offered by the environment naturally limited the range of necessary responses.

Development. Our heaviest baggage from the age of biology is a simple determinism. The Book of Genesis describes the norm for each plant or animal when it predicts each "producing after its kind." "Natural history" was of course a name for the study of these norms—the facts about the reproduction of each species, and especially the "life history" of each species. Just as the butterfly went through the earlier stages of egg, larva, and pupa, so every other organism had its stages. For humankind, moralists in the Middle Ages embellished this with figures of the Seven Ages of Man. And the appealing word "develop" or "development" suggested the essence of this idea. It came into English through the French *développer* and the Old French (from Latin *dis*, reversal, + *voloper*, to wrap up) and signified unrolling or unwrapping. The word implies, of course, that something was already there to be unwrapped, in other words that "development" was the gradual appearance of the expected forms.

There could be no suspense or uncertainty about the next stage in the development of an individual in any particular species. Development could be interrupted and arrested or, on the other hand, nourished and accelerated. Deviation from the path of development was monstrous or miraculous, generally an undesirable departure from the divinely intended role of that species. The concept of *species* embodied and confirmed the path of expectation. A species was by definition a creature that reproduced "after its kind." We have adopted this way of channeling our thought about countries, their cultures, and their economies. We speak of "undeveloped," "underdeveloped," and "developing" countries, which means, of course, that these countries have not yet gone through all the expected, normal (and presumably desirable) stages of "development." We have not yet come to talk of "overdeveloped" countries.

These six Darwinian expectations are our inheritance of vested ideas from an age of biology, when most of the people in Western Europe and North America were still plainly and consciously dependent on the friendly response of nature. The United States Census of 1860, the year after the publication of Darwin's *Origin of Species*, reported that four fifths of the population was still living on farms, and only one fifth was urban (25 million to 6 million). There was yet no city in the United States with as many as one million people. Of the so-called urban population more than half lived in centers of less than fifty thousand. The speedy cityward movement was, of course, one of the strongest currents in American life throughout the next century. By the United States Census of 1970, the proportions of urban and rural were quite reversed, with three quarters urban, and only one quarter rural.

Farm life, too, like the species of plants and animals on which it thrived, tended to reproduce "after its kind." A world of cycles, it was governed by the rhythm of the seasons—spring planting, fall harvest, winter quiet-time for indoor chores. If the rains came, and the sun shone, if snow fell in expected quantity, all would be well. Even the catastrophes were familiar. Drought and flood, blizzard and hurricane and tornado came with dreaded regularity. This dependence on "the elements," on God's disposition of wind and sun and rain, was celebrated by poets and novelists, and even by politicians. "Those who labour in the earth," wrote Thomas Jefferson in his *Notes on the State of Virginia* (1781), "are the chosen people of God, if he ever had a chosen people, whose breasts he has made his peculiar deposit for substantial and genuine virtue. It is the focus in which he keeps alive that sacred fire, which otherwise might escape from the face of the earth. Corruption of morals in the mass of cultivators is a phaenomenon of which no age or nation has furnished an example. It is the mark set on those, who not looking up to heaven, to their own soil and industry, as does the husbandman, for their subsistence, depend for it on the casualties and caprice of customers. . . . the proportion which the aggregate of the other classes of citizens bears in any state to that of its husbandmen, is the proportion of its unsound to its healthy parts. . . ."

Jefferson was still speaking in the accents of the Old Testament prophets, foretelling doom when farmers should no longer dominate the American scene. Ever since his day, American prophecy has been cast in the mold of Darwinian expectations. The vested ideas of Dualism, Conflict, Hierarchy, Displacement, Response, and Development still confine our thinking about the short-term and long-term future. They have become the vocabulary of prophecy, of the ways of our domestic life in the United States and in the West generally, and of our expectations for the nations.

These ways of thinking are no longer relevant. They are in fact dangerously misleading today as we imagine the future. My name for our new situation is the machine kingdom. The obsolete expectations that I have described in this chapter came from the imperatives shaped by natural history, which meant the proverbial animal and vegetable and mineral kingdoms. The fourth kingdom that we have begun to live in during the last two centuries is not the creation of God, of nature, or of slow processes advancing with geologic deliberateness. The machine kingdom is a creation of mankind. It produces some new, even unnatural, problems for our future. And it brings its own erratic, cataclysmic rates of change.

Darwinian expectations have become increasingly irrelevant to modern life in the industrial nations. Yet even as we have emerged from a world of biology into a world of technology, those expectations have survived in some popular contemporary fallacies.

At the heart of these contagious overarching misconceptions is the idea of *species,* central to all thinking about nature both before and after Darwin, but alien to today's world. It is revealed even in our thinking about computers. The word "generation," whose primary meaning has long been the act of procreation, or "offspring having a common parent or parents and constituting a single stage of descent" now is ironically illustrated in the current *American Heritage Dictionary* (1993) in the expression "a new generation of computers." But while the process of procreation, the continuity and regularity of succession found in every "species"—"yielding fruit after his kind" (Gen. Ch. 1)—orders the world of nature, it not only does not prepare us for the ways of technology but actually disorients us.

The units of life are of course self-reproducing. But our machine kingdom is concerned less with *re*production than with production. While much still remains to be explained about the variations in the self-reproducing powers within each living species, we know even less about machine genetics. We know far more about the origin of species than about the origin of the kinds of machines. Though species may show natural selection and the survival of the fittest, the survival of a machine may not be governed by any such rule at all. The crucial intervention of human desires, fashions, advertising, institutions, and whimsies makes it risky to predict survival or procreation on the basis of the intrinsic or genetic characteristics of any particular machine. The promise of survival for a species in nature depends on its ability to adapt to its environment. By contrast, as we shall see, the power of a machine to survive depends on its ability to bring forth its own environment, or create its own demand.

Machines seldom succeed in making earlier machines extinct, even when both the old and the new perform similar functions. The automobile did not succeed in making the bicycle extinct. Where are the dodos of the machine kingdom? Significantly these are less machine types than brand names—the Stutzes and Edsels of yesteryear. Machines drive out other machines for reasons quite different from those of the biological world. Of course machines do not "create after their kind" but spawn other machines of different species. The clothes washer spawns the dryer. In the world of machines, mutation is not the exception but the law. It takes place speedily (with seasonal or annual models), and species commonly interbreed (e.g., the radio and the automobile). The most influential and most widespread machines—the insects of the technological world (such as quartz timepieces, ballpoint pens, mechanical pencils and their combinations and variants, including the latest computer)—become miniaturized and portable. So they are adapted to the most variant conditions, whims, and demands. A distinctive function of the most potent machines is their tendency to assimilate all environments—e.g., the telephone, automobile, radio, TV, Walkman, etc.

The dualism, the dichotomy between the organism and the environment, which seems to govern nature, plainly has no relevance to the world of machines. The "environmentalist" who gives himself the mission of "saving" the environment is speaking an obsolete lingo. Today what environmentalists are really concerned with is not the external dualist counterpart of a "species" of machine, but the very machines that *are* our environment.

The adversary notion, the belief in the universality of conflict, also has no place in our thinking about the machine kingdom. Thomas Hobbes described the state of nature as one of "continual fear and danger of violent death" where the life of man was "solitary, poor, nasty, brutish, and short." He used this truism to justify absolute government. Karl Marx, who saw nature in this same evolutionary mode and saw history as class conflict, translated another truism into his utopian vision of a classless (i.e., species-free) society, attained only by the survival and dictatorship of the "fittest" class (i.e., the "proletariat"). But the legendary law of the jungle, the war of all against all, the battle of the species for survival as the fittest, can only mislead us in the machine kingdom.

The axioms of order—the hierarchy of the world of nature—have also lost their relevance. "And God said, Let us make man in our image, after our likeness: and let them have dominion over the fish of the sea, and over the fowl of the air, and over the cattle, and over all the earth, and over every creeping thing that creepeth upon the earth" (Gen. 1:26). The overwhelming problems of the machine kingdom come from a new ambiguity—between the powers of man and the powers of machines. Having created a machine (an automobile or an atomic weapon), man has created a new force that he is unable either to abolish or to master. Frankenstein is the Mephistopheles of our age. Man's creatures play a novel role. Man can extinguish natural species that menace him—the smallpox or polio virus or some other viruses—or that profit him (the passenger pigeon or whales), but he has never yet found a way to *un*invent the artificial species he has invented.

The irrelevance of the cliché of "response"—of the creation of new kinds of machines to answer predictable and enumerated "needs"—will appear in the next chapters. We will also see the perils of projecting or assuming that the future of institutions in one country will follow the familiar—the "normal"—development in another. But natural history was the distillation of developmental norms—the study of the limits of the probable and the boundaries of the possible.

We see a relic of this attitude in the United States and other democratic countries in the increasingly strident demands that the consequences of each new technology or each new exploration in science be assessed in advance, and proven not to be adverse, before it receives public support, or even before it is allowed to proceed. This movement for legislative endorsement and censorship of progress assumes, of course, that the channels of progress, like the lineage of procreation of species, can be foreseen. But we must recognize a new axiom of our fourth kingdom. "The impossibility of proving impossibilities," as Professor Harvey Brooks puts it, must alert us against Darwinian expectations, against arrogant presumptions of unilinear progress and "development."

The stultifying demands for an unreasonable level of predictive certainty are not the monopoly of any political group. While political conservatives usually "insist on an absolute concept of national security," political liberals tend to "insist on absolute security with respect to safety, health, and environmental problems." Both conservatives and liberals express a traditionally uncritical American faith in technology. Both have smuggled Darwinian expectations, axioms borrowed from the animal and vegetable kingdoms, into our new machine kingdom. Both demand insurance against unimagined progress. Both discourage us from a quest for the peculiar vagrancy of our new world, from a search for the laws of the unexpected.

13

Statistical Expectations

*If you do not expect the unexpected you will not
find it; for it is hard to be sought out, and difficult.*
—Heraclitus (c. 500 B.C.)

It is the unexpected that always happens.
—English proverb

Modern physical science has changed the style of prophecy. We
have moved from qualitative to quantitative prediction. Plato
described the natural course of political development by the
changing qualities of government: honor replaced virtue; wealth
replaced honor. The penultimate evil was democracy—"a
charming form of government full of variety and disorder"
where "subjects are like rulers and rulers like subjects" and "everything is managed by the drones." The cycle would be completed by degeneration into tyranny. Aristotle, too, forecast
cycles in the qualities of government.

The whole advance from ancient to modern science has often
been summed up as a movement from qualities to quantities. It
was heralded in physics by the Newtonian world of numbers, in
physiology by William Harvey's quantitative demonstration of
the circulation of the blood. The social sciences brought persuasive and pretentious prognoses, also with the kudos of numbers.

While Darwinian expectations box us in with axioms of natural history, evolution, and development borrowed from the animal and vegetable kingdoms, statistical expectations have come to confine us in the quantitative categories of the inorganic world, borrowed from the mineral kingdom. "Let us apply to the political and moral sciences," urged the French astronomer Laplace (1749–1827), "the method founded on observation and mathematics that has served so well in the natural sciences." This became the motto for the primer for the modern social sciences, *Social Physics,* by the versatile Belgian astronomer and statistician Quetelet (1796–1874), who, by the way, invented the notion of the "average man." "The more advanced the sciences have become," Quetelet insisted, "the more they have tended to enter the domain of mathematics, which is a sort of center toward which they converge. We can judge of the perfection toward which a science has come by the facility, more or less great, with which it may be approached by calculation."

Today the Cassandras of social science speak the language of numbers. Modern social prophecy has realized Quetelet's hopes. Quantifications give prophetic visions a specious scientific precision. Even the magnitude of mistakes is euphemized as "margins of error." Statistical prophecy is possible, of course, only if we predefine and keep constant the categories of experience—past, present, and future. So we feel enlightened by projections of national product, per capita income, deficits, unemployment, wages, prices, investments, and interest rates. Our economics is a far cry from Aristotle's "management of a household."

The science of statistics thus inevitably conceals the qualitative gulfs between past and future. Karl Marx saw qualities being transformed into quantities. Extrapolation—estimating a quantity beyond the known range on the basis of variables within the known range—is our technique. Assessing the wisdom of costly programs like explorations into outer space usually involves both explicit prediction that the program will produce certain benefits and implicit prediction that it will not produce others.

Still, the largest categories of the unexpected remain beyond quantitative predictions. They are by-products. A by-product theory of history would suggest that the unintended and un-imagined consequences of man's enterprises have been and will always be more potent, more widespread, and more influential than those he intended.

American history plainly shows the significance of by-prod-ucts. The "discovery" of America by Europeans was, of course, quite a surprise. It was an unintended consequence of a search for an expected consequence—a westward sea path to India, Japan, and China. Our presence in the United States is a by-product of the ignorance and miscalculations, courage and ob-stinacy, of some of the greatest navigators in history. We Americans must be forgiven our insistence on the importance of unintended consequences. If fifteenth-century monarchs had been able to foresee how the discovery of America would shatter European certitudes, it is not at all certain that they would have proceeded as they did.

Only the slaves of ideology dare to box in the future. We Americans are congenital anti-determinists. We of all people cannot believe that a straight line is the shortest distance be-tween any two historical points. United States nationalism is a by-product of a war for independence by thirteen quarreling colonies. The peopling of our country is a by-product of the mis-eries of others, of the religious persecutions, the feudal distinc-tions, and class injustices of Europe. The westward movement across our mysterious continent, as often as not, was a quest for what was not there. We are a by-product nation.

When the word "by-product" first came into English usage in the mid-nineteenth century it was appropriately associated with industrial processes. The earliest recorded English use, in Eliza Acton's *English Bread-book* (1857), notes that "German yeast . . . in many distilleries forms an important by-product." The prefix "by-" (as in "byway") had long been an opposite of "main" in describing paths and entrances and passageways, but within the last century it came into common use to describe "a secondary product." Originally the word "product" itself was a term of mathematics, meaning the sum obtained by multiplying two or more quantities together. By the late seventeenth century "product" had begun to mean what was produced by a "natural" process (such as the growth of a plant or the eruption of a volcano). Its etymology is from Latin *pro ducere,* meaning to lead out, bring forth, or extend. Toward the end of the eighteenth century "by-product" began to mean "artificial" products, the result of crafts or skills. The Physiocrats, the influential French economic thinkers, still argued that the crafts, trade, and commerce were all "sterile." Only farmers, they said, were "productive." Since ultimately all production derived from God, the only productive element in the economy was land.

Not until the rise of experimental technology in industrially conscious nations do we encounter the modern concept of a by-product and the pursuit and exploitation of by-products. These, our desk dictionaries now define as secondary or incidental products coming from manufacture. With new forms of artificial power (man imitating God), with the multiplication of manufactured products, by-products also multiply. Research and Development (R&D) becomes a search for by-products, for the hoped-for but unpredictable fruits of a search primarily undertaken for something else.

The familiar early modern examples of historic by-products could be multiplied from more recent history. Galileo was commissioned by the Republic of Venice to develop a military device, "an instrument for seeing at a distance." The consequences of the telescope that shook papal dogma and revised the Western world's view of itself were all, strictly speaking, secondary consequences, merely by-products. Some respected scientists of Galileo's day who had no objection to the military uses of the telescope refused to risk even a glimpse through it of Galileo's "counterfeit" heavens. Similarly, the most productive uses of the microscope turned out to be by-products. Magnifying glasses were first used by Dutch drapers to examine the number and quality of threads in cloth. Antoni van Leeuwenhoek (1632–1723), who had been apprenticed to a cloth merchant and married the daughter of an English serge merchant, had never gone to a university and did not know learned languages. But when he playfully turned the draper's magnifying glass on the waters of a stagnant pond outside Delft, he opened our fantastic vistas of a microscopic new world.

The origins of artificial power are parables of by-productivity. The steam engine began as a device to pump water out of flooding coal mines. Its application to move factory machinery or to propel locomotives was quite incidental. Steam power increased the demand for coal, and at the same time improved machinery for coal mining, which in turn increased the supply of coal, and so brought an age of steam. Electric power also was a by-product—of the lecture-platform entertainments of the eighteenth century, of experiments in electrochemistry, of the search for protection against lightning, and much else. Nuclear power, too, as we all know, was a by-product of the search for an ultimate military weapon. Who can tell what or where will be the next source of artificial power?

Yet the techniques of extrapolation reinforce familiar expectations. Our national economy is measured in gross national product, the well-being of individuals is gauged by personal income, literary products are assessed as best-sellers. Modern marketing seeks new ways to extrapolate the data of polling and sampling to predict consumer demand. Much of the appeal of our strenuous and costly national primary election contests in the United States is their addition of so many new quantitative units and stages and "races"—more data to extrapolate into the crucial election.

Democracy is of course the politics of quantities. It infects us with an insatiable appetite for self-fulfilling prophecies. Hidden within every statistical prediction is an extrapolation—a self-fulfilling prophecy that familiar categories will box in our future. Is this a congenital ill of modern democracy?

The best-seller syndrome and the bandwagon effect could not dominate an uncommunicative society. These special difficulties of reactive democracy in a continentwide electronically equipped nation appeared in the presidential election of 1980. As a consequence of President Carter's premature concession of defeat in Washington in the early evening of the November election day—even before the polls had closed in California—other Democratic candidates complained, many Democratic voters in the West assumed that the race was all over. They failed to go to the polls, and so brought about the extrapolated result that had really not yet happened. The efforts to legislate against the broadcasting of results in the East before the close of the polls in the West have not been successful. Network executives insist on the right of people to know instantly everything the latest technology can bring them. This may be an unresolvable dilemma, a price of freedom.

We may glimpse the perils of our statistical expectations by sampling some known kinds of by-products. We must prepare ourselves for still others.

Expected by-products. We mean here products that are incidental, that we know will come from an activity but that are not its primary purpose. When we build a fire in our fireplace to keep us warm, we know that its by-products are smoke and ashes (which do have a use for us gardeners). With the marketing of the automobile we would expect that a social by-product would be more and better hard-surface roads. Of course our problems come mainly from the automobile's unexpected by-products: the decline of railroads, the rise of traffic jams, parking problems, the dissolution of city centers, "edge-cities," smog, sulfurous pollution of the atmosphere, the visual pollution of used-car lots and automobile cemeteries, murder by drunken drivers, and "carjacking."

By-products that might be expected but cannot be predicted. These are not always undesirable. Experience suggests that oppressive societies, while stultifying their official literature, may produce eloquent literary reactions and creative artistic protests. Were the works of Pushkin and Dostoevsky and Pasternak by-products of tyranny? If so, what does this mean for our national arts and humanities policies? American research and development (R&D) laboratories thrive on expectations of the unpredictable, and are designed to harvest by-products. According to Willis Whitney, the shaping director of the General Electric Research Laboratories (1900–28), these would be the "life insurance" of large industrial enterprises. Whitney, who took over at the age of thirty-two, had an appetite for by-products that the passing years never sated. The job of American engineers, he said, was to produce obsolescence. And obsolescence was another name for the anticipated unexpected. "The gradual goal of good gadgets is gradual obsolescence, or expressed differently, we may get better every day." But research was required because no one could tell for sure where the better might be found. "A director merely points, like some wooden arrow along the highway. . . . the lonely mental pioneer, being grubstaked . . . advances so far into the generally unknown that a so-called director merely happily follows the new ways provided. All new paths both multiply and divide as they proceed."

And, of course, new categories of the unexpected. Our daily life is transformed by technologies for which until recently there was not even a name. These could not possibly have been the result of extrapolation. Examples are the "horseless" carriage (for what later came to be the automobile) and the "wireless" (for what later came to be called radio), which in their very names betrayed popular bewilderment before the unexpected. Atomic "fission" might have been called "splitting the unsplittable." Over the centuries, with only a few exceptions like the medieval town crier and the muezzin who called Muslims to prayer, the technology of communication aimed to send messages to specific addresses. Who would conceivably have paid to send out a message to no one in particular? Radio and television changed all this. The "ratings" of this new technology, and its value as a means of communication, would be determined not by the speed with which it reached some particular addressee but by the copiousness (i.e., the quantity) with which it reached some statistical category. The definition and prediction of these categories by market researchers, opinion pollsters, and political forecasters became a new clairvoyant science and big business.

How can we let the future write its own chapter headings? More than ever we must prepare ourselves for negative discovery—the discovery of new realms of our ignorance, the unwelcome shock that we really know much less than we thought we knew. Arthur Clarke in his *Profiles of the Future: An Inquiry into the Limits of the Possible* (1962) has amplified Harvey Brookes' Law of the Impossibility of Proving Impossibilities. "When a distinguished but elderly scientist states that something is possible," Clarke explains, "he is almost certainly right. When he states that something is impossible, he is very probably wrong." Clarke glosses his word "elderly." "In physics, mathematics and astronautics it means over thirty; in the other disciplines, senile decay is sometimes postponed to the forties. There are, of course, glorious exceptions; but as every researcher just out of college knows, scientists of over fifty are good for nothing but board meetings and should at all costs be kept out of the laboratory!" Despite Clarke's gerontophobe prejudices, he helps us see the professional limits to prophecy.

Arthur Clarke was led to his law by a notorious recent episode in atomic physics. In this case the "elderly scientist" was Lord Rutherford (1871–1937), the brilliant New Zealand physicist who discovered the alpha particle, developed the nuclear theory of atomic structure, pioneered the study of radioactivity, and was deservedly revered as the Newton of his age. Yet he insisted that it would be impossible to unlock and harness the energy that he had revealed to be in the atom. His plausible argument, firmly founded in all that was then known of physics, was a reasonable extrapolation of the laws of the extra-atomic world. Rutherford confidently asserted that it was impossible to initiate a chain reaction that would release more energy than was required to start it. At the meeting of the British Association in Leicester, England, in 1933, Rutherford recalled that it was in Leicester in 1907 that Kelvin had insisted that the atom was the indestructible unit of matter. He discussed recent work on the disintegration of atoms, and went on:

> These transformations of the atom are of extraordinary interest to scientists but we cannot control atomic energy to an extent which would be of any value commercially, and I believe we are not likely ever to be able to do so. A lot of nonsense has been talked about transmutation. Our interest in the matter is purely scientific, and the experiments which are being carried out will help us to a better understanding of the structure of matter.

But in 1934, when Enrico Fermi in Rome succeeded in disintegrating several elements with neutrons, Rutherford had to congratulate him "for escaping from theoretical physics." Five years after Rutherford's death in 1937, precisely such an "impossible" chain reaction was initiated in the squash courts of the University of Chicago. Rutherford believed that his achievement had been to extend the accepted laws of physics to new realms, yet he unwittingly discovered a new Dark Continent.

In the fourth kingdom, then, we must be wary of talking of "evolution" or "development"—and of all predictions based on extrapolation. A more precise word for the past and the future of technology is "expatiation." From Latin *ex,* out of, and *spatiari,* to walk or roam, to "expatiate" originally meant to roam or wander freely—and now helps us see why the destiny of technol-

ogy cannot be packaged in such neat and cheery terms as "evolution," "survival of the fittest," or "natural selection," or by projecting from the tendencies we observe in the present.
Technology advances not progressively but vagrantly.

If Isaac Newton is the beau ideal of the discoverer in modern science, Thomas Alva Edison (1847–1931) is the beau ideal
of the inventor in the machine kingdom. Except for some curious sallies into theology and biblical history, Newton stayed in
the closely related areas of mathematics, physics, astronomy,
and optics. His genius was to encompass countless miscellaneous phenomena in a few grand mathematical generalizations.
Seeking how the universe was held together, he found a way of
assimilating earthly phenomena with the movements of heavenly bodies. Edison's career offered a melodramatic contrast.
His achievements had no theoretical coherence. They were neither the product nor the producer of general theories. At most,
he left a legacy of booster aphorisms on the importance of hard
work, inspiration, luck, and the restless quest for marketable
novelty.

He was himself well aware of the randomness of his accom-
plishments. "A scientific man busies himself with theory," Edison explained in 1888. "He is absolutely impractical. An
inventor is essentially practical. Anything that won't sell I don't
want to invent. Its sale is proof of utility, and utility is success."
Not the least interested in the secrets of the universe, he focused
instead on undiscovered secrets of the marketplace. What might
the conjectural customer buy? Since Edison thought motion pictures were not likely to pay off, he took out only nine patents in
that area. But he was obsessed with the fortunes to be made in
mining, and so obtained sixty-two patents for new techniques of
ore separation. His enormous investments in uneconomic mining devices drove him to the verge of bankruptcy. As his biogra-
pher Robert Conot notes, he shifted his inventive efforts with
the winds of popular enthusiasm—from the telegraph or the telephone to the incandescent light or the X ray, to the electric

automobile, or to the domestic production of rubber. When he happened to start down some line that had not yet captured the public interest—such as the phonograph, wireless telegraphy, or the kinetoscope—he hesitated until there was a clear commercial prospect.

Occasionally, after his inventive appetite was aroused, he might not wait to be assured that his invention would be salable. In 1874, as a young man of twenty-seven, he was trying to invent a telegraph machine that would automatically record the messages received and so make it unnecessary for a telegrapher to be in attendance. He experimented with a stylus marking chemically impregnated paper. Then he found, to his surprise, that if the paper was wrapped around a cylinder and both stylus and cylinder were connected to a battery, the friction of the stylus decreased with the increasing strength of the electric current. In January 1875 he patented this machine, which he called the electromotograph, and he spent the next months trying to find its uses. Edison thought that if he found the right chemical to impregnate the paper, his new machine could actually take the place of the electromagnet then used in telegraphic receivers. This quest took him onto the frontiers of what later proved to be one of the richest of the dark continents of physics, the realm of semiconductors, of transistors and computers. To coat his electromotograph he tried every known element from aluminum to zirconium, and he tested organic substances extracted from fleabane, chickweed, and wild cherries, dandelion and catnip, to mention a few. His laboratory partner Batchelor reported that "after trying some 15262842981 different solutions of Brazilwood we've come to the conclusion that it is not worth a damn." One morning, inspired at breakfast, they actually made a mixture of coffee, eggs, sugar, and milk that produced the report "Phenomenon. Decreased friction on oxygen." But Edison never went on to pursue the wider significance of the curious qualities of semiconductors.

From first to last Edison's quest was random. His 1875 want

list of twenty new processes and products worth inventing included a method of making malleable iron from cast iron; a way to dissolve sawdust in order to provide a cheap substitute for ebony, hard rubber, or celluloid; an oil lamp that would burn without a chimney but would give a bright light; a cheap process for extracting low-grade ores; a sexduplex telegraph; and a cheap process of printing. At his death in 1931 the list of his actual inventions was even more miscellaneous. Besides filling in his early want list, these inventions included telegraphic repeaters, printers, perforators, the mimeograph, an electric pen, the quadruplex telegraph, a musical telephone, a loudspeaker, a phonograph, an incandescent lamp, an improved generator, an electric motor and electric locomotive, ore separators, a cement works, a kinetoscope and motion pictures, an alkaline storage battery, improvements in the typewriter, an autogiro, and countless other items. His patents finally totaled 1,093.

Although Edison was of course a prodigious inventor, he was still only an inventor. After a long life he added almost nothing to our scientific knowledge. The exception, which came to be called the Edison Effect, occurred quite by accident while he was trying to improve his incandescent light bulb. And this story too reveals the limits of his interests. During his experiments in 1883 he was puzzled by the dark shadow that formed inside his light bulb and found that negatively charged particles were emitted from the filament. He did take the trouble to patent this as a device that might have commercial value as a meter. When no immediate commercial use could be found, he abandoned it. But his assistant, John A. Fleming, was tantalized by the problem in physics and pursued it on his own. Through Fleming, the clues that Edison discovered but never followed up actually provided the great physicist J. J. Thomson with data in 1895–97 that helped him to the momentous hypothesis of the existence of the electron. Twenty years later this same clue suggested to Fleming and Marconi the possibility of using a two-element bulb to detect radio waves, and so became an essential lead into the electronic age.

The career of Thomas A. Edison, paragon of inventors in the fourth kingdom, suggests that if there is a law of invention, it is not a law of evolution or linear advance. To expatiate—"to wander freely" and toy with the problem—is the way of the inventor. An investigator inquires systematically and his quarry is the Truth. It is less accurate to call Edison an investigator than a vagrant. He was at play in the world of practical needs, wherever his casual curiosity and the whims of the market led him. The inventor—the Edison on the frontiers of the fourth kingdom—is unconfined by the confident inhibitions of scientific knowledge. In fact it is even misleading to speak of a "frontier"—an outer boundary for the fourth kingdom. That suggests a clear line between the known and the unknown. The seeker in the machine kingdom is not after knowledge but after the novelty whose frontiers are everywhere. "At the time I experimented on the incandescent lamp," Edison confessed or, rather, boasted, "I did not understand Ohm's law. Moreover I do not want to understand Ohm's law. It would prevent me from experimenting."

In our age there is another novel problem, also a by-product of the machine kingdom. When we use the most refined technology to sharpen our statistical expectations we meet the infinite and the infinitesimal. A drastic change in the scale of our thinking about everything has carried more and more of our thought beyond the bounds of our everyday experience. One solace of the biblical view of Creation and of nature was to confine the grandest conundrums in the dimensions of the intelligible. Measurements in palms' breadth and cubits used bodily dimensions, months and years and generations were familiar to all. But the telescope and the microscope, the advances of atomic science, of microbiology and astrophysics, have transformed the popular universe of numbers. No one can experience a light-year. For us laymen the boundary between the finite (or conceivable) and the infinite (the inconceivable) dissolves.

Among the Hottentots, Edward Kasner and James Newman remarked in *Mathematics and the Imagination* (1940), infinity begins at three. "Ask a Hottentot how many cows he owns, and if he has more than three, he'll say 'Many.'" Nowadays we suffer a similar failure of colloquial vocabulary. Our bewilderment begins with a larger number. Our efforts to grasp the now-commonplace quantities of physical science take us beyond the verge. For example, the number of electrons that pass through the filament of an ordinary fifty-watt light bulb in one minute equals the number of drops of water that flow over Niagara Falls in a century. And the number of electrons in a single leaf of a tree is much bigger than the number of pores of all the leaves of all the trees of the whole world. This, we are told, illustrates the crucial difference between a very large number and infinity. "A big number," they say, "is big, but it is definite and it is finite." To help us grasp this distinction Kasner and Newman came up with a new word. Dr. Kasner asked his nine-year-old nephew to think up a name for a very big number, a 1 with one hundred zeros after it. The bright boy suggested "googol." And then, for a still larger number, he offered "googolplex." These authors exercised their own imaginations to help us laymen grasp what such a still-larger number might be. They first suggested that a googolplex should be defined as the number 1 followed by writing zeros until you got tired. But they feared this would not be precise enough because different people get tired at different times. So they finally defined a googolplex as 10 to the googol power, written $10^{10^{100}}$, which equals 10^{googol}. This, they explain, is a "very large but finite number"—an even larger number than all the words that have appeared in the *Congressional Record* of the United States! There would *not* be enough room to write it, if you went to the farthest star, touring all the nebulae and putting down zeros every inch of the way. So we pathetically reach for measuring units of the moon in the familiar dimensions of a football field.

Nowadays we meet a similar difficulty in our efforts to grasp the infinitely small, or the infinitesimal. For two thousand years mathematicians have been plagued by this problem. Zeno's paradox and other puzzles seemed to threaten that the infinitely small could be defined only by denying the very possibility of change and movement. The great mathematician Leibniz (1646–1716) once tried to explain the infinitesimal to his sardonic friend Sophie Charlotte (1668–1705), queen of Prussia (1701–1705), a famous patron of the arts. The queen assured him that she did not need the help of a philosopher or a mathematician, since the behavior of her courtiers had already made her quite familiar with the meaning of the infinitely small. Two centuries later, as Bertrand Russell noted, philosophers and mathematicians "having less acquaintance with the courts, continued to discuss this topic, though without making any advance."

It is more than ever difficult for us laymen to grasp the quantitative meaning of scientific phenomena and social problems. It was back in 1940 that Kasner and Newman were worried over our failure to mark the outer boundary of the finite. The first recorded use in English of the term "atomic bomb" had been in the science fiction of H. G. Wells in 1914. Since then the advances of weaponry, of physics, of astrophysics and microbiology, of supernovas and black holes, of the electron telescope and the electron microscope have brought the infinitely large and the infinitesimally small into the popular discourse of science. Whatever mathematicians may say, the boundaries between the finite and the infinite have become irrelevant and pedantic—as when we are told that the atomic arsenal of the great superpowers has exceeded the destructive power that devastated Hiroshima by more than two hundred thousand times.

Not only in the physical sciences do the quantitative dimensions of our world get out of hand. History begins to take on the dimensions of the infinite. Before the eighteenth century the

Christians of Western Europe were comfortably oriented in chronology by the scholarly reassurances delivered by Archbishop Ussher in 1654. He declared that the Creation recorded in Genesis had occurred on October 26, 4004 B.C. at 9:00 A.M. But archaeology, geology, paleontology, and other sciences have stretched the history of the earth into billions of years, which now exceed our colloquial grasp. Feeble efforts to bring this into our ken tell us that if the whole life of this planet till now were thought of as a single day, the period of man on earth would be only a few minutes. Then, as we reach into the aeons of the universe, we become no more than a nervous glitch in a long feature film. The explorations of the outer universe further tax our imagination.

The figures that we are offered to make experience intelligible become symbols of the increasing incomprehensibility of experience. Take the Library of Congress, for example. Two canonical statistics about our great library are that we catalog books in 468 languages (now, I'm told, 478), and that our receipts come in at the rate of one and a half items for each second of the working year. For the ordinary citizen this can only describe a task of acquisition, cataloging, shelving, preservation, and retrieval that borders on the unimaginable.

So, too, in economics, the sovereign social science of our age. At about the same time that the term "atomic bomb" came into our English language, there appeared the word "macroeconomics," the study of economic affairs in the large, "the over-all dimensions of economic life." Accumulating national and international statistics have increased the quantities handled by the macroeconomist, to the ever-increasing bewilderment of us citizens. While everybody in the United States understands the difference between an 8 percent and an 11 percent interest rate, few of us can usefully grasp the meaning of a $300 billion deficit, or a more than trillion-dollar national budget. Our national budget has become a haunting national problem partly because its dimensions exceed our colloquial understanding. Is it any wonder that we are all tempted to take refuge in the manageable statistics of sports, crime, elections, lotteries, and the stock market?

As the quantitative dimensions of our social problems inflate, we hear plaintive pleas for the "quality" of life. What do we mean by "quality of life" in the United States today? We can do worse than define it as anything and everything that cannot be grasped quantitatively. This would include, of course, faith, love, literacy, art, human fulfillment, history, and life itself. But must we define what is most important for us only in residual terms? Perhaps it is the statistical aspects of life that are the residue. They are self-fulfilling prophecies from which we alone can rescue ourselves.

14

Artificial Selection

*We live in an age when unnecessary
things are our only necessities.*
—Oscar Wilde

Do it the hard way.
—Rube Goldberg

Every animal or vegetable organism has certain limited and de-
finable needs. We can itemize the temperature, rainfall, and alti-
tude at which it will thrive, its nutritive requirements, and the
kind of environment in which it will find shelter, nest, and reproduce. A knowledge of such minimum essentials is required for
all cultivators of the animal and vegetable kingdoms, for the successful gardener, poultry and stock raiser, farmer, or zookeeper.
For man these essentials comprise his "subsistence level"—"the
barest means in terms of food, shelter, and clothing needed to
sustain life."

Of course what makes man human are more than "animal"
needs. And these take us to the frontiers of the indefinable.
Homo sapiens, we call him, from his need to know, which begins to make explicit our inability to limit human needs. When
we also call him *Homo faber,* from his need to make, *Homo
credens,* from his need to believe, or *Homo ludens,* from his
need to play, we are adding the indefinite to the infinite.

What are the consequences of these characteristically human needs for our ability to encompass or imagine our future? All these tendencies converge and are vividly expressed in the fourth kingdom. For the realm of man's own creation dramatizes some crucial differences between the needs of creatures in the animate and vegetative world, and on the other hand the human needs in a world of machines. We have already observed how the process of displacement—pterodons displaced by birds—dominated and appeared to sum up the succession of animal species. Since the biological story of evolution seems to show the substitution of new species ever better suited to the fixed demands of their different environments, and the evolution of new species to fill different environmental niches, we have been ready to assume that a similar displacement occurs in technology. But there is a crucial difference. New machines are only sometimes invented in response to fixed environmental needs. More often man-made novelties are ways of inventing needs.

We Americans are tempted to take a displacive view of technology and social change. We are ready to discard last year's model, for in our country change has often come with dazzling speed. Americans, not uncharitably, have been described as people in a hurry. Ours is the land of the quick lunch. The speedy pace of our life has also brought us fast food, a transcontinental railroad constructed with unprecedented speed, the assembly line, the supermarket, the self-service cafeteria, the drive-in bank, and countless while-you-wait services. We have somehow come to think that all history is a while-you-wait process, which can be completed quickly and before the parking meter has run out. The speed with which new inventions have been devised and new machines marketed has confirmed this view of ourselves. In 1876, there were only some three thousand telephones in the United States, but twenty years later (1897) there were half a million. In 1900 we had only four thousand automobiles, in 1915 nearly a million, in 1916 one and a half million. The first radio broadcasting station was licensed in 1921 and there was only one; in 1923 there were half a million receiving sets, and in 1924 one and a half million. The first television broadcasting station appeared in 1941, when there were only two; in 1948 there were nearly one million receiving sets, and by 1949 there were three million. The multiplication of computers and word processors has more than matched this pace. Fax numbers have suddenly been added to our stationery and business cards. Is there any new technology that Americans will not embrace speedily?

But future events and new technologies never quite fit into cubbyholes of the past. The suspense comes not from wondering what will better perform a familiar function but from wondering what new functions will be invented. It is not a new cast playing old roles, not the television set playing the role of the movies or the radio, but a whole new plot. The machine is a name for an advance into the unknown and the unpredictable as experience ever expands. While others were asking how to breed a better horse, Henry Ford was imagining a horseless world. So the automobile created innumerable novel needs and opportunities (examples: credit cards, shopping centers, suburbs, drive-in banks, etc.). Even if we cannot predict how technology will transform experience, we can confidently say that technology will multiply "needs."

Of course we cannot catalog the unpredictable. But by recalling our experience since the rise of the machine kingdom, we may at least loosen our imagination. We can list a few ways in which new items in the fourth kingdom have affected our experience.

Inventions expand experience. Generally speaking, inventions are additive, catalytic, and expansive. Needs multiply needs. Feedback is the rule and not the exception. The power of an invention is measured by the power and extent of the feedback. An obvious example is the rise and spread of printing and movable type in Western civilization. Before printing, before there were printed books, there was really very little need for books.

In the days of the manuscript book in Europe, a scribe required a full six months to copy a single volume. The largest scriptoria engaged as many as fifty full-time scribes in an establishment that could turn out only about a hundred manuscript volumes in a whole year. Few except clergymen or professional scholars could read. A shop displayed a picture of a boot or a barber's pole, to show what was sold inside, and these have become coveted items of folk art. Illiteracy was so widespread in England in late medieval and early modern times that a legal institution, the so-called benefit of clergy, developed, to provide the religious classes their customary exemption from the jurisdiction of the secular courts. If an accused person was able to read he was legally presumed to be a member of the clerical class and so avoided punishment by the King's courts.

It is hardly an exaggeration to say that printed books created literacy. Books created the demand for books. The printers themselves became a significant new market. In sixteenth- and seventeenth-century Europe, when printing made Bibles and religious tracts cheaper and more widely available, newly literate congregations were more suspicious of their priestly intermediaries. They wanted to read and interpret sacred texts for themselves, and this, with other factors, helped bring about the Protestant Reformation, and widespread secession from the Roman Catholic Church. By the mid-eighteenth century, inexpensive mass-produced books had midwifed new forms of literature. Novels were now being written by Richardson, Fielding, Smollett, and others, appealing to women, who were learning to read, and were becoming book buyers. By the nineteenth century, cheaper paper and improvements in the press brought the mass-circulating newspapers and magazines for a population of mass readers. And daily newspapers, of course, increased the need for still-cheaper paper and speedier presses.

When the written word became the printed word its feedback expanded and transformed experience in surprising ways. The standardized pagination of the printed book made possible a standardized index, which made it easier for readers to look up references and check sources. Now they could see whether the books really said what the priests and professors said they said, and all readers were better qualified to appeal to the "authorities" against authority. While this diffused printed versions of some sacred learned texts, such as Galen on anatomy, and so perpetuated his errors, it also provided a common focus and a common body of learning for the whole enlarged literate community. Vernacular languages brought a vernacular literature and helped create nations. For readers everywhere, printed books widened horizons, which meant, of course, a new fellowship with ancient poets, philosophers, and historians, and with contemporaries in distant places, a wide-angle lens on the world.

Inventions redefine experience. They create new units and new boundaries between the parts of experience. They increase the needs for the machines that create new virtues, new vices, new benefits, and new commodities. There is no better example of the power of technological feedback than the clock. The inventing and manufacturing of clocks created the need and demand for clocks. Until lots of people owned or had access to timepieces there was obviously little need for anyone to have one. Why be there "on time" if nobody else was?

One of the surprising facts of technology is that for most of human history people had only the crudest ways of measuring time. The clock does not enter the lives of European communities until the late Middle Ages. Then it appears first to mark the times of religious services. The oldest surviving mechanical clock, at Salisbury Cathedral in England, dates from about 1380. In ancient times there were no mechanical clocks that we know of, and people had to tell time by the sundial (useful only during the day and when there was sun) or by the sands of the hourglass or by the water clock. The great church clocks and town-hall clocks were a form of public works, like the water supply or a drainage or sewage facility, providing the time when there was no other way of knowing it.

Until the nineteenth century owning a clock was a sign of wealth, and the watch was even scarcer, essentially a form of jewelry. In the eighteenth century, therefore, there was a different sense of time. When someone called on George Washington or Thomas Jefferson he was on time if he came within fifteen minutes or half an hour of when he was expected. Punctuality could hardly be a virtue when most people lacked the means of being punctual. Benjamin Franklin listed in his *Autobiography* the twelve martinet virtues in which, working at one each month, he hoped to perfect himself. But he did not list punctuality, since there was no way of enforcing it. The young United States of America attracted the wonder of the world with its cheap dollar watch (made by applying Eli Whitney's principle of interchangeable parts), and it was no accident then that this also became the land of the quick lunch and of young men in a hurry.

Just as the clock redefined chronological experience, so the camera redefined visual experience. There is the familiar story of the mother who was walking her baby in the park when her friend exclaimed in admiration at the beauty of the infant. "That's nothing," the proud mother replied, "you ought to see his photograph!" The prevalence of cameras, of course, creates the need for cameras. No self-respecting father would be without a photograph of his children, nor without a camera to keep the record of their growth. For an actress now it is less important to be beautiful than to be "photogenic" (a word that first appears in English about 1928). And for the tourist nothing else is quite as essential as a camera.

Inventions create penumbras. The old distinctions in experience are dissolved or fogged over. New borderline areas are created, confounding the most obvious commonsense distinctions—between past and present, the spontaneous and the reproduced, the dead and the living. A television watcher is seldom certain whether what he is watching is "live" or taped, the moviegoer need not know whether the actor he sees on the screen is in fact living or dead. When we phone an airline or a museum for information, it is not always clear whether the answer comes from a spontaneous human voice or a "recorded message." The rise of photography, phonography, motion pictures, television, and other electronic media is the climax of this ambiguity-creating power of machines. The VCR (videocassette recorder) and its competitors remove the last vestiges of the time definition of broadcast experience.

Inventions are irreversible. Since no one has ever invented a way of *un*inventing or *dis*inventing a machine or ensuring its extinction, needs for machines can only multiply. The multiplication of automobiles increases the need for public transportation—for buses, subways, and airplanes—yet somehow this does not reduce the demand for automobiles. As automobiles make it possible for us to reach more and more places where we cannot park, this simply increases the need for parking places, parking meters, and parking garages again without reducing the demand for automobiles.

Inventions are increasingly intrusive. The advance of technology in our time attests our increasing inability to exclude novelties or their consequences from our daily lives. The excreta of automobiles make it harder and more dangerous to breathe in great urban areas. Television is, of course, another example. In the past parents worried over how to bring home to their children the messages that they believed to be desirable. Now they must try to "ration" the television experience that is already in the living room. Willy-nilly, the experience pours in, and the hard question is how to stop the flow. One desperate optimist, anxious for some sense of control, is cheered to "think of all the commercials, old movies, Westerns, politicians, comedians, quiz shows, soap operas and other intrusions we can keep out of our home just by turning off one little knob." (The multiplication of cable channels gives each of us a grand new power of exclusion.) But more and more families now have that knob in every room, and it seems much easier to turn it on than to turn it off. All the momentous proliferations of technology—from the automobile to the computer—can be chronicled by their increasing intrusion into the interstices of our daily lives.

What GNP does not measure is the expanding output of *wants*. The United States, imperfectly described as a land of unprecedented wealth, could equally be called the land of unprecedented *wants*. Our nation has grown by its need for the unnecessary—another name for human progress. Perhaps we might better measure our advance not by some quantitative index of "productivity"—of gross national product—but by some qualitative index of proliferating "needs."

In the fourth kingdom, are there laws like natural selection and the survival of the fittest that were supposed to govern the multiplication of plants and animals? Can we ever predict the vitality or longevity of particular machines? According to Thomas Malthus, because populations multiply geometrically and the food supply multiplies arithmetically there is an ever-increasing need to control or reduce the human population. Darwin and Wallace observed that in any given environment a struggle for existence had to go on because the means of subsistence were limited and increasing numbers of organisms were competing. Old species were dying, and new species emerging. Then over time there would be a relatively constant population in any given environment, for the unlucky or the unfit were no longer there.

In the fourth kingdom, the machine kingdom, such limiting conditions no longer exist. The "environment," which for living organisms provided only limited and finite subsistence, has now become indefinitely, even infinitely, expandable for machines. Human "needs" have no limit, and they are never satisfied. In the natural world, man sometimes intervenes by "artificial selection," by controlled breeding or by hybridizing, or by eliminating weeds or predators or inferior offspring. Sometimes, of course, as with passenger pigeons, whooping cranes, tigers, or whales, man's intervention can endanger or extinguish a whole species. Still, in nature this is the exception rather than the rule, and on our planet as a whole the processes of natural selection, the competition for limited resources in an environment, go on, producing the dominance of some species, the decline or extermination of others.

But in the machine kingdom, artificial selection is the rule. The Malthusian equation is reversed. For machines subsist on human wants or "needs." And these increase geometrically, responding to the increase of machines that is also geometrical. New machines create new "needs" and new needs produce new machines. The survival of any particular machine, then, is determined by a combination of the qualities of the machine itself and the effectiveness of the additional machinery for awakening that need, that is, by advertising. In a free society, where inventors and developers and manufacturers and merchandisers are relatively free to catalyze the "need," the most effective advertisement for any new machine is the machine itself. Advertisements for the automobile or the radio or television or the computer proved weak stimulants of demand compared with the experience of riding in an automobile, hearing the radio, watching a neighbor's television set, or trying a computer.

The curse of original sin, for which Adam and Eve were driven from the Garden of Eden, was the progenitor of the labor theory of value. "In the sweat of thy face shalt thou eat bread," God warned Adam, "till thou return unto the ground" (Gen. 3:19). So man's effort to reduce his labor—to reduce the sweat of his brow—or to make labor more tolerable, has seemed a way of redeeming himself from the curse of original sin. Materialist and economic interpretations of history have tended to assume that man's desire to escape from labor was the motive force in human history. Yet John Stuart Mill wisely doubted whether "all mechanical inventions yet made have lightened the day's toil of any human being." Karl Marx took off from what he considered a truism to explain why modern machinery and steam power would make life ever more intolerable, would multiply miseries, and so in the long run would lead to revolutions, toward a withering away of private property and the state. But the old distinctions between idleness (which Marx liked to use to characterize the owners of the means of production) and labor became elusive and hard to apply in a world of machines. For example, as Ruth Schwartz Cowan has shown in *More Work for Mother,* the elaborating technology of the household, far from reducing the workload for the middle-class American house-wife, has simply changed the workload, made it more multiplex and complicated. And the prospects for the housewife are not unique.

All this means that to prepare ourselves for the future we must find a new vocabulary for the unexpected. We must free our-selves from Darwinian expectations and statistical expectations, and at long last face man's capacity and his tendency to invent problems. We must be prepared for the vagrancy of inventions and the infinity of needs. Inherited slogans must be revised or reversed. Among the old saws that we inherit from the farmer's age, the age of biology, one of the most familiar is that "neces-sity is the mother of invention." This comes to us from the time when man ransacked his environment to meet basic animal needs. Human technology was treated as only a higher version of the chimpanzee learning to use a stick to knock down bana-nas to feed his stomach. But in our machine kingdom we have lost our very ability to define or to limit the elements of animal survival. However much we may talk of "survival," in the United States only a small and unfortunate number of us know the meaning of subsistence. The American economy is domi-nated not by food production but by the production (or nonpro-duction) of automobiles, of electronic devices, of nuclear and other sophisticated machinery of warfare, by their raw materi-als, their servicing, and their obsolescence. Though the tech-nologies of warfare undeniably become ever more potent means of destruction, the technologies of peace preoccupy us with nonessentials. And these are the hallmark of a "developed" soci-ety. For us, invention has become the mother of necessity.

. . .

Are there any new axioms to describe what we may expect in the machine kingdom? Recognizing, as we must today, that man is a problem-inventing animal, our vision of the future must be as open-ended as knowledge, as random as play, as surprising as human imagination and ingenuity. Yet it may not be impossible, by following a few cautionary maxims, to prepare ourselves better for the unexpected. The few following axioms are clues not to the limits of futurity, but to the limits of prophecy. They may give us some handles on the unpredictable.

It is impossible to prove impossibilities. Our predictions must never rest on the assumption that anything can*not* be done. "My experience," Thomas A. Edison recalled late in life, "is that for every problem that the Lord has made me he has also made a solution. If you and I can't find the solution, then let's honestly admit that you and I are damn fools, but why blame it on the Lord?" What was more axiomatic than that the voices and moving images of the living would die with them?

Technology advances vagrantly. Who can tell what technological challenge, what everyday task, what flight of fancy will next engage some bold inventor? Machines compound machines whose by-products are still more unpredicted machines, and even more unpredicted machines to make them—each of which may have countless random by-products. The automobile helped produce the modern assembly line. Who can guess what the assembly line might help us produce?

Technology elaborates. There is no task that cannot be done by a more complicated machine. Not Charles Darwin or Frederick Taylor but Rube Goldberg is the true prophet of our machine kingdom. "Do it the hard way!" The survival of any nonhuman organism may well be governed by its economy of means and by its efficiency in a given environment. Physical processes may be governed by a law of entropy that degenerates and so reduces available energy. But the creative forces of the machine kingdom multiply with elaboration. For man, "needs" multiply needs, and call forth new ingenuities. Inventive powers are always in excess of invented needs. Each elaboration spawns other elaborations, and the pace accelerates.

The viability of a machine depends on its capacity to create its own need and to bring forth the environment that makes it necessary: the law of artificial selection. Therefore the appeal and survival power of any machine cannot be estimated until the machine itself exists. A machine's longevity then depends on its continuing ability, nourished by newly competing machines, to form mutants, to create and serve ever-newer needs. Miniaturization homogenizes environments and multiplies environmental needs. With the Walkman and its spinoffs we wear more and more of our environment and make it mobile.

Technology becomes ever more unintelligible to us users. As customers increase and the pace of elaboration quickens, the knowledge gap widens between, on one side, those who make and maintain the machines and, on the other side, us the customers. As technological powers grow, the knowledge grasp of the citizen declines. Can we, should we, become resigned to the deepening mystery of daily life?

15

The Great Separation

*Science is a first-rate piece of furniture
for a man's upper chamber if he has common
sense on the ground floor.*
—Oliver Wendell Holmes,
The Poet at the Breakfast-Table

In the founding years of our American republic at the end of the eighteenth century the wise and learned John Adams described the puzzlement that we still feel. "In so general a refinement or more properly a reformation of manners and improvement in science," he asked in 1786, "is it not unaccountable that the knowledge of the principles and construction of free governments in which the happiness of life and the further progress of improvement in education and society and knowledge and virtue are so deeply interested—is it not unaccountable that these should have remained at full stand for two or three thousand years?" He added that "the principles of political science were as well understood at the time of the neighing of the horse of Darius as they are at this hour."

In that very next year, 1787, when John Adams was in Britain as the new nation's ambassador, the fifty-five men who met at Independence Hall in Philadelphia between May 25 and September 17 would invent new federal representative institutions in the bright light of modern history. Both the manner of creation and the product were unprecedented and the viability of this American Constitution would be no less surprising.

John Adams's dour observation, which he intended also as a prediction was, of course, wrong. The history of his own time showed that what he called "the principles and construction of free governments" would and could improve. Elsewhere in Western civilization and in other parts of the world the nineteenth century revealed remarkable progress in political technology. What Adams might have observed more precisely was a process of divergence, what I would call the great separation, between science and technology on the one hand and political and social institutions on the other.

To understand our problem, we must begin by accepting the fact that progress is not monolithic. The interesting and urgent question arises not because mankind does progress in science but does not progress in political institutions. Rather it arises from the divergence of the several ways in which the progress occurs.

Scientific progress and technological innovation have both been marked by the increasing acceptance of paradox. The English word "paradox," of course, derives from a Greek word, *para,* meaning beyond and *dox,* meaning common opinion. For example, the primitive mind seems to have found it difficult to accept the fact that you could cross the stream and still not get wet. Then man discovered that by using a floating object or building a bridge, he could cross the stream and still stay dry. This simple paradox is a model for many if not most of the important advances in our scientific and technological thinking.

There are two features, then, to a paradox. First, it is a seemingly contradictory statement that may nonetheless be true and, second, it is contrary to the generally received opinion. Our mastery of the physical world comes, of course, from our increasing willingness to accept a paradox. Is there a single significant step forward in science that did not have these two paradoxical characteristics when it was first proposed? This helps us understand why the great discoverers have had such trouble in getting their ideas adopted and why discoverers have so often been persecuted by the respectable authorities of their time.

Inventors have had similar problems, and the more radical and innovative their inventions, the greater their troubles. The popular abhorrence of paradox has been as fierce in technology as in science. When Thomas A. Edison described his electric generator and his new system for distributing current to make his electric lighting scheme workable, one leading scientist exclaimed that it would be a public calamity if Mr. Edison should waste his great talent in such puerility. What was considered the most ridiculous feature of this system was his proposal to run electric motors on the same circuit as electric lights.

Nearly three centuries earlier, as we have seen, Galileo had faced similar objections to his "instrument for seeing at a distance." Some eminent contemporaries simply refused to look through his telescope. Others insisted that though it might work on the earth, when turned on the heavens it was surely deceiving them. Another of Galileo's epochal observations after his legendary dropping of objects from the Leaning Tower of Pisa— that bodies do not fall with velocities proportionate to their weight—was also, of course, a paradox. His telescope had opened a whole world of paradoxes. There were lots of things in the heavens that we could not see with our eyes. Then could God really have intended for us to see them at all? Was it possible that the heavenly bodies were not what they seemed, that the Milky Way actually was only countless separate stars—and so on?

The microscope, of course, opened still another paradoxical world of invisible objects. Centuries would pass before the commonsense notions of spontaneous generation would be conquered by that general acceptance of belief in minute organisms that most of us have never seen and probably will never see.

The most flagrantly paradoxical of the advances of modern

science are, of course, in atomic physics. We laymen find it hard to believe that every solid object around us, including this paper, is not really solid at all, but consists of countless constellations of atoms, each of which is mostly empty space with parts in constant motion. This is our version of the fifteenth- to seventeenth-century scientific revolution that showed the earth itself in motion around the sun and led John Donne to lament "all coherence gone."

From the very beginning the advance of civilization has depended on the acceptance of paradox. The progress of communication, the invention of writing that put sounds on stone or clay or animal skins or papyrus, also made it possible to hear the words spoken by those far out of earshot and even by the dead. Modern communication simply elaborates those paradoxes so that sounds and moving images can travel on wires or even without wires across oceans and continents through solid walls and to and from moving vehicles. The progress of transportation, too, is, of course, marked by paradox—a vehicle pulled without an ox or a horse, or flying through the air in vehicles heavier than air. All this is obvious.

There is no denying that science and technology bring us the fruits of paradox. Our advanced industrial society delivers the fruits into our daily lives. Perhaps we laymen are so little troubled by this because, as Max Frisch observed, technology is "the knack of so arranging the world that we don't have to experience it." The progress of civilization dulls our feeling for paradox. We lose our capacity to wonder. We are no longer awed by the surprising and the unfamiliar. We become less exclamatory and less poetic.

But we cannot leave the matter there. At the same time that the advances of science and technology permeate our consciousness with paradox, another powerful modern movement surrounds us in the West—the progress of common sense. This produces a troublesome modern social schizophrenia. The Greek philosophers, led by Aristotle, developed an idea of common sense with a technical, psychological meaning. For Aristotle, common sense was a kind of mental switchboard, a human faculty in which the various reports of the several senses are reduced to the unity of a common apperception. It was a master sense, a common bond of the five senses, where these were reduced to a unity of consciousness.

Over the last centuries this usage has declined, and in its place, along with the rise of liberalism, of representative government, and of public opinion, in our English language common sense has acquired a new, more colloquial meaning. It has become one of our most widely used expressions in public debate.

"Common sense" now has two aspects, both contrary to the features of paradox. First, it means sound practical judgment that is independent of specialized knowledge, the verdict of normal native intelligence. A homely American synonym is "horse sense." Secondly, it means also the prevailing or majority view. This is related to the medieval use of *communis sensus*—the sense of common humanity or fellow-feeling found in most people.

These two meanings, native good judgment and the majority opinion, have become increasingly intertwined and inseparable. Common sense made a spectacular debut in the Western political scene in the American justification of the American Revolution. When some people said that the Declaration of Independence of 1776 had not one new idea in it, its author, Thomas Jefferson, did not deny the charge. On the contrary, Jefferson said the purpose of the document was not to find out new principles or new arguments never before thought of, not merely to say things that had never been said before, but as Jefferson said, "to place before mankind the common sense of the subject."

This was the very phrase that Thomas Paine had made the title for his powerful pamphlet that same year, espousing the American Revolution. Paine's purpose, of course, was to persuade everybody by implying that the American cause was what everybody already believed and could not help believing. It was simply "common sense." But when Paine used this phrase, he was slightly premature. He did not dare sign the pamphlet. His friend Dr. Benjamin Rush, a prosperous physician and a pioneer psychiatrist, had persuaded Paine to write the pamphlet because Rush feared that his own medical practice might suffer if he was publicly associated with ideas that had not yet quite become common sense.

Liberal institutions and representative government have been championed since the seventeenth century as vehicles of the rising influence of ordinary good sense against priestly mysteries and kingly unction. Jefferson believed that the revolution which made the United States of America possible was just another episode in the inevitable surge of intelligible, publicly justifiable, publicly acceptable government institutions endorsed by the majority—that is, commonsense government.

Modern political technology has increased the articulateness, the definiteness, and the power of majority-view common sense. For example, in the spread of literacy, of public education, of daily newspapers and speed presses, the rise of the secret ballot, the widening of the suffrage, the rise of market research and opinion polling, and a whole new branch of science called psephology, the rise of the so-called sunshine laws in Washington to open the records of government to public scrutiny and the judgments of common sense, and ethical disclosure requirements for public officials, along with the rise of radio and television broadcasting. All these have increased publicity and public accountability to common sense for government officials.

Demagogues—Shakespeare's "many great men who have flattered the people, who ne'er loved them"—became ever more difficult to identify when popularity, direct appeal to public feelings, became the main avenue to political power. But while the power of "public opinion," the modern democratic term for common sense, increases in politics, the divergence from scien tific and technological realms of paradox becomes wider and wider.

As we the public increasingly delight and luxuriate in the everyday miracles of science and technology that pass our understanding, we still demand an ever-tighter commonsense rein on political power. What are the consequences of this divergence in our way of thinking?

Historically, as we have noted, common sense, the accepted majority view, has been the instant enemy and the vocal antagonist of the great discoveries in science. When the English book publisher John Murray sent the manuscript of Darwin's *Origin of Species* to the Reverend Whitwell Elwin, the distinguished editor of the prestigious *Quarterly Review,* Elwin advised against publication. The subject, he said, was too controversial. Elwin, who had a feeling for the opinion of the times, urged that instead Darwin should write a book about pigeons, on which Darwin was reputed to have some very interesting ideas. "Everyone is interested in pigeons," he wrote in his report, which has become a classic in publishers' annals. "The book would be reviewed in every journal in the kingdom, and would soon be on every library table." Luckily, Darwin was not persuaded. We have already noted the perils of requiring from our technology the advance assurances it cannot give and which apparently the Reverend Elwin wanted to receive—the danger of remaining blind to the impossibility of proving impossibilities.

But we are no better today than we ever were at predicting the directions of science and technology. The most important innovations will always be the unpredictable ones, such as discovering that the axiomatically unbreakable is not only breakable but explosive. Yet the more common sense dominates our political institutions, the more stridently it will demand just such impossible assurances. The dictatorship of common sense demands insurance against the unexpected as the price of public support and as a ransom against legal prohibition. Today more than ever we can be grateful that progress is not monolithic, that there are different kinds and categories of thought and institutions, each with its peculiar laws or lawlessness.

The powers of common sense in popular government are naturally inclined to oppose the powers of paradox. Our storehouse of paradox—another name for our treasury of scientific knowledge—is, of course, cumulative. On the other hand, the wisdom of majorities, the complacent dogmatism of common sense, being not a resource but an attitude, is not cumulative. The wisdom of majorities does not add up to anything unless it be the growing arrogance of growing power.

In our time, the commonsense majority—through opinion polls and at the ballot box—watches over and exercises a veto on the governmental decisions that few of the majority can understand. The machines of war, the very names of which are a mystery to the citizens, have become decreasingly intelligible even as the budget of defense becomes an increasing proportion of our national budget.

Progress on which our standard of living and our national survival depend requires an unpopular tolerance and encouragement of the puzzling enterprises of science and technology, from nuclear energy to genetic engineering. This disparity grows. The ultimate test of our democratic society may be our power to allow the progress of paradox in science as we defer to common sense in our society.

VI

A PERSONAL
POSTSCRIPT

16

My Father, Lawyer Sam Boorstin

I never knew anyone quite like my father, but then I never really knew my father, either. He was a man without a single vice, but with a hundred foibles. He was a "devoted" husband in a miserably unhappy marriage. He was embarrassingly proud of me and advertised my small academic triumphs by stopping fellow Tulsans on the street to show them newspaper clippings, and he thermofaxed my letters home to give to passing acquaintances. Yet he never once praised me to my face. When I won my Rhodes Scholarship to go from Harvard to Oxford, he had no comment, but noted that a neighbor boy had been given a scholarship to send him from Tulsa Central High to the University of Oklahoma. My mother was one of the world's best cooks, not in the gourmet category, but in the Russian Jewish style, spending endless hours in the kitchen to make her cheesecake or her blintzes just right. Then when my father came to dinner from his office (always later than expected) he seldom failed to say that he "would just as soon eat a bale of hay. . . . Man should eat to live, and not live to eat."

Still, there was never any doubt that my mother ruled the roost, and her tribal feelings confined the family's social life. For most of our years in Tulsa we lived in a duplex apartment, with my mother's sister Kate and her husband and daughter living below. My mother's only friend was this sister, but my father was everybody's friend and spent his spare hours in the lobby of the Tulsa Hotel, and later the Mayo Hotel, chatting with acquaintances or strangers or simply reading the newspaper and hoping to be interrupted by a strange or friendly voice. My mother was suspicious of anyone who was not a blood relation (including especially her brothers' wives), while my father's suspicions (with some reason) fell especially on the blood relations themselves.

Except for two or three occasions when we entertained at dinner a local merchant who was my father's prize client, I cannot remember a single occasion when we had nonfamily guests in our house or were in another Tulsa home. Everything about our life—including our coming to Tulsa—seemed dominated by my mother's family. I never understood how two people so ill suited to each other could ever have married. But the story of how my father and mother first met was supposed to explain it. And behind that was the story of the last years of my father's independence, back in Atlanta.

My father always spoke with a warm and soft Georgia accent. His father was one of the many Jews who emigrated from the Russian pale in the late 1880s to escape pogroms, military service, and persecution. This Benjamin Boorstin came on his own and for some reason, never explained, settled in Monroe, Georgia. His brother came about the same time. But the immigration officers spelled his brother's name Boorstein, and so he remained. The two brothers had stores on opposite sides of the street in Monroe, where their differences of name were constant reminders of their recent arrival. Benjamin Boorstin sent for his wife, who came over with their infant, Sam. My father went to school in Monroe. While working in a general store in his spare time he managed to collect the premium tags attached to the little bags of cigarette tobacco he was selling. He sent off a stack of these tags and received one of the primitive plate cameras.

This camera changed his life, for he used it to earn his way through college. Arriving in Athens, Georgia, the site of the state university, he quickly found his way into the office of the president. He showed the president his photographs of the cracked walls and peeling ceilings of the university classrooms. These pictures, and more like them, he said, would persuade the state legislature to grant appropriations for repairs and for new university buildings. With that he applied for the novel job of university photographer and got it on the spot. Then he worked his way through by helping the president with his campaign for larger appropriations and by taking class pictures.

In those days law was an undergraduate subject. When Sam Boorstin received his LL.B. degree he was still under twenty-one, and when he appeared before the judge to be admitted to the bar, it was objected that he was under age. He won his first case when he persuaded the judge to admit him anyway, and so became the youngest member of the Georgia bar. In Atlanta he began practice as junior member of one of the most prestigious old law firms. He spent his spare time joining every fraternal organization that would let him in. These included the Elks, the Odd Fellows, the Red Men, and the Masons. I still have the fine Hamilton gold watch with the Masonic emblem engraved on the back that was given to him when he became the youngest Worshipful Master in the United States. He kept his hand in as a beginner in Georgia Democratic politics, which became easier when Governor John Marshall Slaton engaged him as his private secretary. One of Sam Boorstin's qualifications—in addition to personal charm and an outgoing manner—was his elegant handwriting. He had acquired a beautifully rotund and flourishing hand by attending a penmanship school. His flamboyant signature was one of the first mannerisms that I tried to imitate—without any success.

He might have had a career in Georgia politics, even though he was a Jew. But unpleasant events surrounding the infamous Leo Frank case intervened and made this impossible. In 1913 the innocent pencil manufacturer Leo Frank was railroaded on a charge of raping and murdering one of his employees in a turbulent trial that roused the ugliest passions of racism and anti-Semitism that Georgia had ever seen. The case became a newspaper sensation. My father, though still one of the most junior members of the bar, lent a local hand to the defense, as aide to several eminent imported Eastern lawyers, including the distinguished Louis Marshall. When, to no one's surprise, Frank was convicted, my father had the bitter assignment of carrying that word to Frank's wife. In 1915, after his death sentence was reduced to life imprisonment by the courageous Governor Slaton, Frank was seized and lynched by a raging mob, who had the shamelessness to have their photographs taken standing proudly beside the dangling body of the innocent Frank.

There followed in Atlanta one of the worst pogroms ever known in an American city, an unpleasant reminder of the Russia from which the Boorstin-Boorstein brothers had fled. My mother's brothers then owned a men's clothing store in Atlanta, whose store windows, like those of other Jewish merchants, were smashed in the aftermath of the Frank case. The prospects were not good for a young Jewish lawyer interested in politics.

Meanwhile, in 1912, my father had married my mother under legendary circumstances. She had come down from New York City to visit her brothers in Atlanta. The handsome and promising Sam Boorstin began courting the attractive Dora Olsan from the "East." The society section of the *Atlanta Constitution* carried a picture of the pretty visitor with the story of a dinner held at the hotel in her honor. Governor Slaton was present, and at the end of the dinner he arose, offered a toast, and said, "Sam Boorstin, if you don't marry that beautiful girl, I'll see that you're disbarred." Sam married Dora.

The Frank case impelled my mother's three brothers—along with my father and the husband of her sister—to leave Atlanta. They went to Tulsa (then still pronounced Tulsy), Oklahoma, a

frontier town in what only nine years before had still been Indian Territory, set aside for the so-called Five Civilized Tribes.
In 1916 Tulsa had few paved streets and fewer paved sidewalks.
My three uncles opened a bank, and the husbands of the two
sisters tagged along, with Kate's husband joining the bank. My
father opened a law office, slightly separating himself from the
family, and he soon became one of Tulsa's most energetic boosters.

After settling in Tulsa—which my mother despised (and never
stopped despising)—my father never really took a vacation. He
made a few business trips and once came to England to visit me
when I was at Oxford. But he thought Tulsa was a good enough
year-round place. My mother (usually with her sister) left town
at the first crack of summer heat, usually to go to Atlantic City
or some other resort.

It is still hard for me to understand—much less explain—my
father's love affair with Tulsa. He thought, or at least said, it
was the greatest place on earth. In fact, Tulsa was a frontier
village translated into the architecture and folkways of the
1920s. With endless prairies stretching around, there was no
good reason for skyscrapers. Still, Tulsa built the Philtower, the
Philcade, and the Exchange National Bank Building, all of
which cast their twenty-two-story shadows across the barren
plain.

As for culture, there wasn't much. Only a Carnegie library,
the annual visit of the Metropolitan Opera Company—heavily
sponsored by the best ladies' "ready-to-wear" clothing stores—
and Kendall College, a Baptist missionary school to which none
of the wealthy local citizens sent their sons and daughters.

My father joined in the manic optimism for the future of
Tulsa, which soon called itself the Oil Capital of the World. Oil
was mother's milk to all of us raised in Tulsa. And the gambling
spirit infected my uncles, who played for, and won and lost,

fortunes in oil. Would their next well be a "gusher" or a "dry hole"? Was it possible to open a new "oil field" on this or that farmer's land? This was the adult jargon most familiar to me.

While my father was a booster for Tulsa, he never became an oil gambler. Instead he became a species of lawyer now nearly obsolete. He was a lone "general practitioner." He never had a partner (my mother would not have tolerated it), but through his office came a stream of young lawyers just out of law school whom he trained in the old apprentice style. They adored him, but found him difficult to work for. Many of them became district attorneys and judges, or they founded prosperous law firms that far outshone his own. He had his own way—his very own way—of doing everything. This included the way you use an index, the way you hold a pen, the way you talk to clients. Each of these apprentices stayed for a few years and then went on— much wiser in the law and how to practice it, but relieved at not being told how to do everything. I personally suffered more than once from my father's insistence on doing things his way. After I had been shaving for many years my father still insisted on my running the razor against the grain of my facial hair, as "the only way to get a close shave." His golf lessons, offered in a warm spirit of paternal helpfulness, made me hate the game, and I've never gone near a golf course since.

My father would have been happy to see a SAMUEL A. BOORSTIN AND SON shingle outside his office, and to that end he really hoped I would go to the University of Oklahoma. My mother's insistence that "only the best" was good enough and that I must "go East" to Harvard helped save me from all that.

Still, my father's law practice was exemplary for those who believe that the law is a public-service profession. The big money was in oil, and he had a share of corporate oil practice. But what he enjoyed most, and talked about most, was his "general" practice. This was more like the work of a village curate than of a city lawyer. He was especially proud of the occasion when he saved a hapless girl from disaster. He prevailed on her mother not to seek annulment of a quickie marriage until several months had passed—and so ensure the legitimacy and the financial provision for the baby he wisely suspected was on the way. This despite the mother's and the girl's protests that "nothing had happened." There were countless occasions when he prevailed on irate husbands and wives not to go for a divorce. And there was the time when he helped secure the acquittal of one of his clients on a murder charge for shooting a rival merchant on Main Street.

As a prominent Democrat he was naturally the best general counsel for the *Tulsa Tribune,* an outspoken, right-wing Republican daily. He defended the *Tribune* against numerous libel suits, and despite their sometimes provocative postures, he never lost a case for them.

He never got rich in the practice, but he had one profitable piece of good luck. A representative of Amtorg (the Soviet oil combine), who had come to Tulsa to improve his knowledge of oil-well technology, was run over by a truck and had to spend weeks in a local hospital. My father took his case and won one of the largest personal-injury verdicts on record in Tulsa at that time. The damages awarded were in the neighborhood of seventy-five thousand dollars. This was by far my father's biggest case—which somehow gave me a warm feeling for the Soviet Union. But from a family point of view there was a price to pay. I don't think my father ever told my mother how much of a fee he had received in this case. But I do remember my mother's frequent question: "Whatever happened to all the Kapalushnikov money?"

My father's law office was a piece of Americana. The place of honor went to a pen-and-ink drawing of a mythical judge representing the Majesty of the Law—which my father had had me trace from a picture that impressed him—and a photograph of the justices of the hallowed Supreme Court of the United States. On the walls and under the glass on his desk were mottoes, uplifting aphorisms, and lines of verse. The most poignant message (and now the most obsolete) in those days of breach-of-promise suits was the framed commandment: "Do Right and Fear No Man; Don't Write and Fear No Woman." There were some Edgar Guest poems and Kipling's "If—" in an ornate version printed by Elbert Hubbard's press. And then: "When the One Great Scorer comes to write against your name—He writes—not that you won or lost—but how you played the game." His favorite modern literature was Elbert Hubbard's "A Message to Garcia."

My father still seems to me to have been the most unmercenary man in the world. He took cases because he thought he could somehow help someone. He never pressed for his fees and took cases without thinking whether the client could ever pay him—which of course infuriated my mother. He also loved to give gifts, and never worried about the cost. There was a particular kind of loose-leaf address book bound in leather that he thought (and insisted) everyone should use. If a celebrity came to lecture at Town Hall, afterward he would send him one of these books and try to begin a correspondence. Each address book must have cost over ten dollars and they added up. He treasured the letters of acknowledgment he received from the celebrities, which he pasted in a book and showed to visitors to his office.

His law practice required a good deal of reading—in the extensive law library that he maintained in his office. He invited other lawyers—especially the young ones just beginning—to use freely this library, which must have been one of the best and most up-to-date law libraries in town. His nonlegal reading was myopically focused. If he found a book that he really liked he would give it biblical status. One particular biography of Judah P. Benjamin—the first professing Jew elected to the U.S. Senate (1852–61), who held high office in the Confederate States of America and at the end of the war emigrated to England, where he prospered as a barrister—caught his fancy. He never failed to refer to it whenever any question of history or literature arose, and pressed me to read and reread it.

He was an early champion of gummed and printed name stickers and Scotch tape, which he affixed to everything— books, golf clubs, hats, tennis rackets. He could never under- stand why I preferred the pristine book. This was only one expression of his love of gadgets, his booster faith in the newest way to do anything, including laxatives and the latest electronic belts and exercise machines to cure all ills. As an optimist he was a ready victim for visiting book salesmen and their multivolume subscription sets, often in "simulated leather." I remember par- ticularly the unbroken (and mostly unopened) sets behind the glass doors of our living-room bookcase, which included the *Works of Theodore Roosevelt, The World's Great Orations, Beacon Lights of History,* and the speeches and writings of the notorious atheist Robert G. Ingersoll.

My father's enthusiasm for Robert G. Ingersoll did not inter- fere in the least with his public stance as a Jew. We were mem- bers of all three Jewish synagogues—the Orthodox on the impecunious North Side and the Orthodox and Reform syna- gogues on the prosperous South Side. My father was active in the Anti-Defamation League and in various interfaith activities. But I can never remember his presence at a religious service. Very different from my paternal grandfather was my mother's father, who lived with us for many years and was scrupulously Orthodox. Jacob Olsan went to shul every day, did no work on Saturdays, and was the reason for our maintaining a kosher kitchen with a separate set of dishes for Passover. The status of Jews in Tulsa was curious. Tulsa was a headquarters of the Ku Klux Klan, which was responsible for burning down the Negro sections of town in one of the worst race riots of the 1920s. The Klan had no patience for Tulsa Jews, but the Jews somehow paid little attention to their gibes. My father and his Jewish friends looked down condescendingly on them and their like as a bunch of "yokels."

I don't know how much life in Tulsa had to do with it. But just as my father was totally without vice—he never smoked, drank, or to my knowledge womanized—so he was an irritatingly tolerant man in his opinions. I could never get him to express an adverse or uncharitable judgment on anyone—including the Klan bigots and the rising Nazis. He always tried to make allowances for why people did what they did. He was a living example of how immigrant, mobile, westward-moving Americans wore off the edges of their convictions—how the West saved some people from bigotry but provided a fallow ground for bigots. I will never forget his contagious enthusiasm for the novelties of American life, and for the undocumented halcyon future.

17

Land of the Unexpected

With a Europe in disarray, in a century plagued by two murderous world wars, by genocides without precedent—the German Nazi massacre of six million and the Stalin-Soviet massacre of thirty million—how can I speak hopefully about the American future?

One answer is very personal. I was raised and went to public school in the 1920s in Tulsa, Oklahoma, which then called itself the Oil Capital of the World, but could perhaps have been called the Optimism Capital of the World. Only ten years before my family came to Oklahoma, the Indian Territory had been admitted to the Union as the forty-sixth state. The city thrived on "booster" pride, and before I graduated from Central High School it boasted two daily newspapers, three skyscrapers, houses designed by Frank Lloyd Wright, and a public school system superintended by the former U.S. commissioner of education. The Kiwanis, Rotary, and Chamber of Commerce competed furiously in projects of civic improvement. For our high school English classes we memorized and declaimed patriotic orations—from Patrick Henry's "Give Me Liberty or Give Me Death" and Lincoln's Gettysburg Address to Henry Grady's "New South" and Émile Zola's "Plea for Dreyfus." We wrote speeches on the virtues of the federal constitution for a national contest that held its finals before the Supreme Court in Washington. Of course there were dark shadows—such as the relentless racial segregation, the brutal race riots of the 1920s, and the Ku Klux Klan. But these were not visible or prominent in my life. The city burgeoned, proudly built a grand new railroad depot, a university, and an elegant public library and city hall—and soon it was embellished by art museums of national rank.

My father was one of the most enthusiastic boosters and the growing city seemed to justify his extravagant optimism. I came to sympathize with that American-frontier newspaperman who was attacked for reporting as facts the mythic marvels of his upstart pioneer village, including its still-unbuilt impressive hotel and prosperous Main Street. In America, he said, it was not fair to object to the rosy reports of community boosters simply because they had "not yet gone through the formality of taking place." I suppose I have never been cured of my distinctively American Oklahoma optimism, bred in the bone and confirmed by the real history of Tulsa.

Another answer is in American history. The exhilarating features of our history and culture have in the past been captured in the idea of American Exceptionalism. This is a long word for a simple idea—the traditional belief that the United States is a very special place, unique in crucial ways. It is symbolized in our national capitol in Washington, which proclaims our European heritage in the elegant classical motifs of its dome. But the dome is held together by a triumph of pioneer technology, a hidden cast-iron frame, which in its making provided the needed employment for American workers. American Exceptionalism is a name too for a cosmopolitan, optimist, and humanist view of history—that the modern world, while profiting from the European inheritance, need not be imprisoned in Old World molds, nor limited by the ancient raw materials of community. And therefore that the future of the United States and of the people who came here need not be governed by the same expectations or plagued by the same problems that had afflicted people elsewhere.

How have we lost sight of this beacon? We have been seduced by the rise of our country as a "superpower." For power is quantitative, but the uniqueness of the United States is not merely quantitative. We have suffered, too, from the consequences of our freedom. Totalitarian societies exaggerate their virtues. But free societies like ours somehow seize the temptation to exaggerate their vices. The negativism of our press and television reporting are of course the best evidence of our freedom to scrutinize ourselves. Far better this than the chauvinism of self-righteousness, which has been the death of totalitarian empires in our time.

While nations of the Old World have enjoyed their legendary heroes shrouded in historic mists, our nation was founded in the bright light of history. They have embroidered glowing myths of Romulus and Remus, Joan of Arc, Saint Louis, and Richard the Lionhearted. But our founders—our John Smith, William Bradford, John Winthrop, Benjamin Franklin, George Washington, and Thomas Jefferson—are vividly and conspicuously human. So they remind us, to our benefit, of the human origin of all institutions. But our founders become ready targets for journalistic history. We see Jefferson depicted as a philanderer and Lincoln degraded from the Great Emancipator to a small-town lawyer. So, too, the achievements of recent presidents are overshadowed by docudramas of bedroom peccadilloes.

The founders of our nation were well aware of the uniqueness of their situation and sought inspiration in the uncanny novelties of America—past, present, and future. Even before the American Revolution, Benjamin Franklin organized an American Philosophical Society in Philadelphia, to explore the unpredicted promise of this unknown continent. In his Circular Letter of 1743 Franklin sketched their open-ended concerns: "All new-discovered Plants, Herbs, Trees, Roots . . . New Methods of Curing or Preventing Diseases. All new-discovered Fossils . . . New and useful Improvements in any Branch of Mathematicks; New Discoveries in Chemistry . . . New Mechanical Inventions for Saving labour . . . All new Arts, Trades, Manufactures, &c . . . New Methods of Improving the Breed of useful Animals . . . New Improvements in Planting, Gardening, Clearing Land, &c . . ." Thomas Jefferson himself, president of the society and its inspired leader (1796–1815), believed that here at last the happiness of the human species might advance "to an indefinite, although not to an infinite degree."

We must never forget that while to the Old World we were the Unexpected Land, we have ever since been the Land of the Unexpected. The main features of the culture of our United States are just what the wise men of Europe, looking at their own past, could not have conjured up. A short list of the American surprises includes what we have done here with four basic elements of culture—religion, language, law, and wealth.

Take religion as a starter. By the time of the European settlement of North America the history of the rising nations of Western Europe had been punctuated by torture and massacre in the name of religion. There was the notorious Spanish Inquisition of the fifteenth century, in France the bloody Massacre of St.Bartholomew (1572), and in Germany during the very years of the Puritan settlements in New England the Thirty Years' War (1618–48), which spread into a general conflict between Protestant and Catholic Europe. In that war alone some 10 percent of the German population was slaughtered in the name of religious orthodoxy. This seemed not to augur well for a nation like ours, whose Pilgrims were obsessed by religion and had fled England to fulfill their passionate dream. Their religious faith gave them courage to brave the ocean crossing, the hardships of an unknown land, and the risks of hostile natives, despite their lonely remoteness from ancestral homes.

Who could have predicted that the United States, unlike the nations from which our people came, would never suffer a religious war? That the Protestants and Catholics who had tortured and massacred each other in Europe would establish peaceful neighboring communities from New England to Maryland and

Virginia? That Jews would here find asylum from ghettos and pogroms? And that, though the United States would remain conspicuously a nation of churchgoers, the separation of Church and State would become a cornerstone of civic life? Or that public school principals in the twentieth century would be challenged by how to promote a holiday spirit without seeming to favor or neglect Christmas, Hanukkah, or Kwanza?

In Europe, languages had made nations. Spanish, Portuguese, English, French, German, and Italian had produced their own literature even before there was a Spain, a Portugal, an England, a France, a Germany, or an Italy. But the United States would be the first great modern nation without its own language. Our country has been uniquely created by people willing and able to borrow a language. Oddly enough, the English language has thus helped make us a congenitally multicultural nation, since most Americans have not come from the land of Shakespeare. So we have learned here that people do not lose their civic dignity by speaking the language of a new community. The English language has been invigorated and Americanized by countless importations of words from German, Italian, French, Spanish, Yiddish, and American Indian tongues, among others. With the surprising result that without a national language unique to the United States, our community has developed a language wonderfully expressive of the vitality and variety of our people. Perhaps we should really call Broken English our distinctive American language, for it bears the mark of our immigrant history.

Nowadays we can be puzzled at the spectacle of peoples from Russia to South Africa contending over how, whether, and when to adopt a "constitution." They seem to have the odd notion that a "constitution" can be created instantly by vote of a legislature or by a popular election. All this offers a sharp contrast to our Anglo-American experience. The tradition of a fundamental law—a "constitution"—that we inherited from England reached back to at least the thirteenth century. The by-product of a nation's whole history, the unwritten English constitution was a pillar of government and of the people's rights. No one could have foreseen that such a tradition would find a transatlantic written reincarnation in the deliberations of fifty-five colonials meeting in Independence Hall in Philadelphia in 1787. So our United States was created by a constitution. With another surprising result—that our parvenu nation at the end of the twentieth century now lives by the most venerable (and probably most venerated) written constitution in the world. And that the Constitution would survive by its very power to be amended (with difficulty).

Yet who could have predicted that a nation whose birth certificate bore the declaration that "all men are created equal" should have been one of the last to abolish slavery? In 1772 Lord Mansfield in the famous Somerset's Case held that any slave would become free on landing in England. Then slavery was abolished in the British Empire in 1834. Still, three decades passed before Lincoln's Emancipation Proclamation of 1863 freed slaves in the Southern secessionist states, followed by the Thirteenth Amendment (1865) to the Constitution outlawing slavery in all the United States. The slave trade survived only in certain Muslim states and in parts of Africa.

On the other side, we must note that our only civil war was fought in a struggle to free a subject people. For this, too, it is hard to find a precedent. And a legacy of the history of slavery in the United States has been the equally unprecedented phenomenon of a conscience-wracked nation. Which has led us to create a host of novel institutions—"equal opportunity" laws, "affirmative action," among others—in our strenuous effort to compensate for past injustices.

We should not be surprised that Russians are obsessively suspicious of foreigners coming to their country—after their long domination by the Mongols, their invasion by Napoleon and his forces of "liberation" who burned Moscow, and by the Germans in World War II who left twenty million casualties. No wonder they see the foreigner as the invader or the agent of invaders. We have been luckily free of this stereotype in the United States and instead have inherited the vision of other newcomers refracted in the experience of our own recent immigrant ancestors. "Strangers are welcome," Benjamin Franklin explained in his *Information to Those Who Would Remove to America* (1782), "because there is room enough for them all, and therefore the old inhabitants are not jealous of them." This has been the mainstream of our history—welcoming the newcomer as worker, customer, community builder, fellow-citizen-in-the-making. The uniquely American notion of a nation of nations was never more vivid than today.

We are told that the United States is a *rich* nation. But what really distinguishes us is less our wealth than our radically novel way of measuring a society's material well-being. "Wealth," which was at the center of English mercantilist thinking before the American Revolution, was a static notion. The wealth of the world, measured primarily in gold and silver treasure, was supposed to be a fixed quantity—a pie that could be sliced one way or another. But the size of the pie could not be substantially increased. A bigger slice for Great Britain meant a smaller slice for France or Spain or somebody else, and one nation's gain was another's loss. Our New World changed that way of thinking. People have come here not for wealth but for a better "way of life." America bred a vaguer and more expansive view of the material world, and blurred the boundary between the material and the spiritual. All this was reinforced by the spectacular progress of our technology, exploiting the resources of a rich, little-known, and sparsely populated continent.

The American Revolution, then, was among other things a struggle between the time-honored idea of Wealth and a New World idea of Standard of Living. This characteristically American idea appears to have entered our language only at the beginning of this century. It could hardly have been conceived in an Old World burdened with the legacy of feudal "rights," landed aristocracies, royal courts, sacrosanct guild monopolies, and ancestral cemeteries. Wealth is what someone possesses, but a Standard of Living is what people share. Wealth can be secretly hoarded, but a Standard of Living can only be publicly enjoyed. For it is the level of goods, housing, services, health, comfort, and education agreed to be appropriate.

All these remarkable transformations of the culture of the Older World add up to American Exceptionalism. This is quite the opposite of Isolationism—"the Dracula of American foreign policy." "We shall nobly save or meanly lose the last, best hope of earth" was Lincoln's way, in the heat of our Civil War, of declaring the nation's unique mission to the world. More recently we have heard apologies for such expressions of belief in American uniqueness, as if it were somehow provincial or chauvinist. But our ex-colonial nation in this postcolonial age would do well to see what the prescient French man of letters André Malraux observed on his visit to President Kennedy in the White House in 1962, which is still true. "The United States is today the country that assumes the destiny of man. . . . For the first time a country has become the world's leader without achieving this through conquest, and it is strange to think that for thousands of years one single country has found power while seeking only justice." And, he might have added, "while seeking community." We must see the unique power of the United States, then, not as the power of power, but as the power of example. Another name for history.

The depressing spectacle today of a Europe at war with itself has offered us a melodrama of those same ghosts of ethnic, racial, and religious hate that generations of immigrants have come to America to escape. Now more than ever we must inoculate ourselves against these latent perils. Luckily, the states of our federal union are not ethnic, racial, or religious enclaves. Luckily, we have remained a wonderfully mobile people. There is no better antidote to these perils than a frank and vivid recognition of the uniqueness of our history—of the special opportunities offered us. Nor could there be a greater folly than refusing to enjoy the happy accidents of our history.

The uniqueness that Jefferson and Lincoln claimed for us, we must remember, was for the sake of all mankind. Our Declaration of Independence takes its clue from "the course of human events." The Great Seal of the United States on our dollar bill still proclaims "Novus Ordo Seclorum"—a new order of the centuries. When before had people put so much faith in the unexpected?

Acknowledgments

These recent essays, originally published as indicated below, have been revised for this volume.

Chapter 1. "The Age of Negative Discovery," keynote address to the World Space Congress in Washington, D.C., on August 31, 1992, as "Realms of Discovery, Old and New," and published in the proceedings of that meeting by the American Institute of Aeronautics and Astronautics. Copyright © 1992, by Daniel J. Boorstin. The observations by Marc Davis are drawn from his lecture at the California Institute of Technology, November 15, 1991, published in the Bulletin of the American Academy of Arts and Sciences, May 1992, at p. 64.

Chapter 2. "The Cultures of Pride and Awe," introductory chapter, entitled "Realms of Pride and Awe," in the National Gallery of Art Catalogue to the exhibit "Circa 1492," Washington, D.C. Copyright © 1991, by Daniel J. Boorstin.

Chapter 3. "An Odd Couple: Discoverers and Inventors," from *Inventors and Discoverers* (National Geographic Society, 1988), reprinted by permission.

Chapter 4. "The Writer as Conscience of the World," keynote address to the Jerusalem International Book Fair, April 20, 1993, reprinted in *The Aspen Institute Quarterly,* Autumn 1993. Copyright © 1993, by Daniel J. Boorstin.

Chapter 5. "Our Conscience-Wracked Nation," from the 150th anniversary edition of *The Economist* (London, September 11, 1993) as "A Conscience-Racked Nation," reprinted by permission.

Chapter 6. "Printing and the Constitution," from *Constitution of the United States: Published for the Bicentennial of Its Adoption in 1787* (The Library of Congress in association with the Arion Press, San Francisco, 1987).

Chapter 7. "Roles of the President's House," keynote address on the 200th anniversary of the White House, at the Willard Hotel, Washington, D.C., October 13, 1992, published in *The White House, The First Two Hundred Years* (Northeastern University Press, 1993). Copyright © 1992, by Daniel J. Boorstin.

Chapter 8. "The Making of a Capitol," introduction to *The United States Capitol* (Stewart, Tabori & Chang, 1993). Copyright © 1993, by Daniel J. Boorstin.

Chapter 9. "An Un-American Capital," from "Compromis, passions et protestations," introduction to *Des Villes en Amerique: Washington* (Autrement, Paris, 1987).

Chapter 10. "Tocqueville's America," introduction to Alexis de Tocqueville, *Democracy in America,* 2 vols. (New York: Vintage Books, 1990). Copyright © 1990, by Daniel J. Boorstin.

Chapter 11. "Custine's Russia," foreword to Marquis de Custine, *Empire of the Czar* (Doubleday, 1989). Copyright © 1989, by Daniel J. Boorstin.

Chapters 12, 13, 14, and 15, "The Fourth Kingdom," are adapted from my Ishizaka Lectures in Tokyo, delivered under the general title "The American Future: The Fourth Kingdom and the Limits of Prophecy," and published in a Japanese-English edition by the Simul Press (Tokyo, 1986). Copyright © 1986, by Daniel J. Boorstin. In Chapter 12, the phrase from Harvey Brooks is taken from his lecture in the Herbert Spencer Series on Technology and Society, at the University of Pennsylvania on April 14, 1976.

Chapter 16. "My Father, Lawyer Sam Boorstin," from *Family Portraits,* ed. Carolyn Anthony (Doubleday, 1989). Copyright © 1989, by Daniel J. Boorstin.

Chapter 17. "Land of the Unexpected," from *Parade,* July 10, 1944. Copyright © 1994, by Daniel J. Boorstin.

For friendly and sage editorial advice I am again indebted to my Random House editor, Robert D. Loomis.

All these essays had the advantage, before their original publication, of the counsel and encouragement of my incomparable companion and principal editor, Ruth F. Boorstin, who conceived and edited this volume.

Index

ABOUT THE AUTHOR

DANIEL J. BOORSTIN, the Librarian of Congress Emeritus, is one of our nation's most eminent and widely read historians, author of the bestselling *The Discoverers,* now translated into over twenty languages, and *The Creators.* His celebrated earlier trilogy, *The Americans,* was awarded the Pulitzer, Bancroft, and Parkman prizes. He has won the Dexter Prize of the Society for the History of Technology, the Watson Davis Prize of the History of Science Society, and the National Book Award for lifetime contribution to letters.

He directed the Library of Congress for twelve years. Before that he was Director of the National Museum of American History of the Smithsonian Institution, and earlier had been the Morton Distinguished Service Professor at the University of Chicago, where he taught for twenty-five years.

Born in Georgia and raised in Oklahoma, he received his B.A. *summa cum laude* from Harvard and his doctor's degree from Yale and is a member of the Massachusetts bar. He has spent a good deal of his life viewing America from the outside, first in England, where he won a coveted "double first" while a Rhodes Scholar at Balliol College, Oxford, and was admitted as a barrister-at-law of the Inner Temple, London, and more recently as a professor in Rome, Paris, Cambridge, Kyoto, and Geneva. He has lectured all over the world, and has been decorated by the governments of France, Belgium, Portugal, and Japan. He died in 2004.

Printed in the United States
by Baker & Taylor Publisher Services